"This book tells the truth about poisons like pesticides and poison producing plants. They cause irreversible harm to people and nature. To read this book is a must. It is a wake up call for parents and all of us to defend the health of especially small children and the basis of our future, which is nature."

Renate Künast MdB, elected member of the German parliament
and former German minister agriculture

"André Leu's powerful book is the ideal antidote to the pernicious propaganda that has deluded so many governments, farmers, and consumers into believing that synthetic pesticides are not only safe but necessary. Through extensive evidence and compelling reasoning, it conclusively demonstrates that these chemicals are unacceptably risky and utterly unneeded. And although it's alarming, it is ultimately inspiring, because it reveals that we can produce abundant and nutritious food for everyone on earth through natural, organic practices that don't poison our bodies and our environment — and that regenerate our soil while reducing the excess carbon in our atmosphere."

Steven M. Druker, J.D. author of Altered Genes, Twisted Truth

"Poisoning our children" is essential reading for anyone alive who wants to thrive and stay healthy. Andre Leu has written an in-depth guide to the world of pesticides and chemicals and how to know what the labeling means. We are under the greatest environmental assault in the history of humanity. To not educate yourself is to accept the conditions and diseases that are afflicting so many. You will read and then refer to this book for years to come. This book should be in every household in America and the world."

Suzanne Somers, actress and author of Tox-Sick From Toxic to
Not Sick *and numerous New York Times bestsellers on wellness and health*

"It's time for parents to realize that an entire generation of our children's potential, their health, intelligence and reproductive organs are being compromised by toxic chemicals. We can protect our children. Read this book."

Zen Honeycutt, founder and director, Moms Across America, mom of three
boys, speaker, writer, artist, lover of natural healing and wife

POISONING
OUR
CHILDREN

POISONING
OUR CHILDREN

The Parent's Guide to the
Myths of Safe Pesticides

ANDRÉ LEU

ACRES U.S.A.
GREELEY, COLORADO

POISONING OUR CHILDREN

Copyright © 2018, André Leu

Acres U.S.A.
P.O. Box 1690
Greeley, Colorado 80632 U.S.A.
970-392-4464
info@acresusa.com • www.acresusa.com

Printed in the United States of America

Cover design by Malisa Samsel; special thanks to Afton Pospisilova.
Interior design by Sarah Marshall and Mary Stephens McGinnis.

Front cover photography used under license from Povareshka/iStock/Getty Images.
Roundup® and Roundup Ready® are registered trademarks of Monsanto Company.

Publisher's Cataloging-in-Publication
André Leu, 1953–
Poisoning our children / André Leu. Greeley, CO, ACRES U.S.A., 2018
xxx, 198 pp., 23 cm.
Includes bibliographical references, index, tables, and illustrations
ISBN 978-1-601-73140-1 (print edition)
ISBN 978-1-601-73085-5 (ebook edition)
1. Pesticides—Health aspects. 2. Pesticide residues in food. 3. Spraying and dusting residues in agriculture. 4. Pesticides—Environmental aspects.
I. Leu, André, 1953– II. Title.
TD887.P45L48 2018 632.95042

Dedication

To my wife Julia: for more than 40 years of love and partnership in our various adventures. They would not have succeeded without your support. We still have many more adventures to look forward to.

To our sons Asha and Nick: you grew up on the impossible farm. I was told that I could never introduce the new crops that we grew to Australia. After I did that, I was told it was impossible to grow them organically. The experts also told me that it would be impossible to sell them as we were too far from the main markets. The impossible takes a bit longer and more planning. Never let people tell you that your dreams are impossible. Dream on, plan and be persistent — you'll get there. Dreams do come true.

To my brother Michael: our parents gave us extraordinary childhoods that have resulted in lifetimes of adventure — some failed, others prospered, especially now, as we are both doing well at this latter part of our lives. We have that special bond between brothers — a deep and enjoyable friendship.

To Alan and Suzi Carle: for 45 years of continuous friendship and showing that it is possible to save an enormous amount of endangered biodiversity, educate many thousands of people about it and be a profitable farm.

To all the affiliates, board members and staff of IFOAM Organics International: I regard being President is the greatest honor that an organic farmer can have — better than a Nobel Prize. Thank you for your support and trust in me.

Contents

About the Author

André Leu is a founding member and director of Regeneration International. He served as president of IFOAM Organics International from 2011 to 2017. He is the author of the award-winning book, *The Myths of Safe Pesticides*.

He has an extensive knowledge of farming and environmental systems across Asia, Europe, the Americas, Africa and Australasia from over 40 years of visiting and working in over 100 countries.

André has a degree in communications and post-graduate qualifications in adult education. He lectures and teaches at many universities, institutions and workshops around the world. He speaks at numerous conferences, seminars, and workshops, as well as United Nations events on every continent. He meets with governments, industry, farmers, consumers, and NGOs on the multi-functional benefits of regenerative organic agriculture.

His work has been published extensively in magazines, newspapers, journals, conference proceedings, newsletters, websites, and other media.

André and his wife Julia run a regenerative organic, agroecological tropical fruit orchard in Daintree, Queensland, Australia. In his spare time he grows tropical plants, particularly waterlilies and plays and writes music on guitar and keyboards. He used to be a professional musician, but now he just plays for fun.

Foreword

I write this foreword from Cordoba, Argentina, which has become the epicenter of transgenic soya, and with it the spraying of glyphosate, a herbicide, also sold under Monsanto's brand name Roundup.

Three hundred million liters of glyphosate are being sprayed annually. That translates into five liters per person — the highest in the world. Cordoba is also the epicenter of a health crisis and children are paying the highest price. Cancer rates and birth defects have exploded. Six to seven percent of the children being born suffer from malformations.

André Leu's *Poisoning Our Children* is an urgent wake-up call to the world. It brings us the latest research on the disease epidemic unleashed by poisons in our food. But it does more. It shows that poison-free alternatives work better both in controlling pests and in producing healthy, nutritious food. There is no justification for staying on the pesticide treadmill.

Pesticides and herbicides are poisons. We need to start naming them honestly. André has done that. And we need honest science to assess both their impact on our children's health and on their necessity in food production.

As André Leu shows, scientific studies and people's practices are finally establishing that agroecology and organic farming produce more and better food which is poison-free. The International Assessment of Agricultural Knowledge, Science (IAASTD), the Intergovernmental Panel on Climate Change (IPCC) of agriculture, has concluded that neither the Green Revolution based on chemicals, nor the gene revolution based on GMOs, is producing more food. But the poisons are causing severe and irreversible harm to the planet and people, especially our small and fragile children. Cancers, neurological problems, and digestive tract problems are exploding exponentially.

And this epidemic can only be addressed through a systems causality assessing the impact of the poison complex on complex living systems. Linear and mechanistic causation is inadequate for the task.

Conflict of interest makes the risk assessment of poisons and the search for solutions worse. When those who cause the disease with their poisons also decide what is safe and what is not, our children are not safe from hazards.

When the giant poison industry can go after every independent scientist, from Arpad Putzai, to Gilles-Éric Séralini, to Tyrone Hayes and Ignacio Chapela, science itself is under threat. Corporations like Monsanto know what harm they cause, and suppress it, as in the case of the carcinogenic properties of glyphosate. Monsanto knows.

And the same corporations that sell the poisons for agriculture, and patented GMOs, also sell the patented cancer drugs. For them the harm to us and our children is creating new market opportunities.

With the merger announced between Bayer and Monsanto, the issue of corporate power over our food and health, and the issue of corporate accountability become even more urgent as a democratic imperative.

Monsanto and Bayer have a long history. They made explosives and lethally poisonous gases using shared technologies and sold them to both sides of both the World Wars. Bayer was part of IG Farben, Hitler's economic power and pre-war Germany's highest foreign exchange earner, with offices in the United States and Switzerland.

Monsanto entered into a joint venture with IG Farben, Hitler's supplier of Zyklon-B, a cyanide based pesticide used in concentration camps during the holocaust. Zyklon-B was used as evidence in the Nuremberg trials, finding IG Farben guilty of war crimes. Monsanto and Bayer also had a Joint Venture — MOBAY. Mobay supplied ingredients for Agent Orange in the Vietnam War. Twenty million gallons of Mobay defoliants and herbicides were sprayed over South Vietnam. Children have been born with birth defects, and adults have chronic illnesses and cancers, due to their exposure to Mobay's chemicals. Monsanto and Bayer's cross-licensed Agent Orange resistance has also been cross developed for decades. Wars were fought, lives were lost, countries carved into holy lands — with artificial boundaries that suit colonization and resource grabs — while Bayer and Monsanto sold chemicals as bombs and poisons.

More recently, according to Monsanto's website, Bayer Crop-Science AG and Monsanto Co. have "entered into a series of long-term business and licensing agreements related to key enabling agricultural technologies." This gives Monsanto and Bayer free access to each other's herbicide and the paired herbicide resistance technology. Through cross-licensing agreements like these, mergers and acquisitions, the biotech industry has become the IG Farben of today, with Monsanto in the cockpit. Monsanto's attempted buyout of Syngenta would have merely been an accounting and liability-reduction exercise within the much larger conglomerate of industrial chemical agriculture and biotechnology. There is no competition between Big Ag and biotech corporations. In India, even the distribution channels of chemicals, seeds and the credit farmers take to buy these toxics, are the same for Bayer and Monsanto.

Monsanto's website states the following about the long-term agreements:

1. Within the framework of these agreements Bayer Crop Science will grant Monsanto a royalty bearing, non-exclusive license for its LibertyLink® herbicide tolerance technology for use in corn and soybeans, the two largest field crops in terms of acreage in the United States. The agreements provide Monsanto with an option to market corn and soybean seeds which contain both Monsanto's Roundup Ready® and Bayer CropScience's LibertyLink® technologies, which could provide farmers with additional weed management solutions. Monsanto and Bayer Crop-Science also amended certain existing agreements in the area of herbicide tolerance to provide each other more favorable terms.

2. In the area of insect resistance, the two companies have also entered into a royalty-bearing agreement giving Bayer CropScience rights under certain Monsanto intellectual property. In addition, the companies amended other agreements related to insect-protection technologies, including Monsanto's existing non-exclusive, royalty-bearing license for use of Bayer CropScience's Dual Bt technology. This enables Monsanto to commercialize products containing multiple insect resistance genes with different modes of action.

3. As part of the agreements, Monsanto and Bayer CropScience cross-licensed each other under their respective patent estates for RNAi technology, an important enabling technology for the development of new agricultural products.

Monsanto's Bt technology, licensed to Bayer, has failed miserably in India. Cotton crops have been decimated because of the failure of Bt-cotton. Farmers in Punjab have lost almost all their crops, and the debts of the planting season hang around their necks.

As the Bt Crop was failing, Bayer saw an opportunity. Through questionable means, Bayer persuaded the state of Punjab to buy its pesticide Oberon as a solution to the white fly epidemic, selling over 33 crores (330 million Rupees — about $5 million) worth of Oberon to desperate farmers with the aid of the Agriculture Department. The Oberon scam has left the following Bayer cronies, from the Agriculture Department of Punjab, charge sheeted: Agriculture Director Mangal Singh Sandhu, Joint Director Agriculture Balwinder Singh Sohal and the Deputy Director (Cotton) Parminder Singh. They have been charged under section 420 (cheating), section 409 (criminal breach of trust), 120 B (criminal conspiracy) and under section 13 (2) read with section (13 (1) (d) of the Prevention of Corruption Act, 1988. Bayer has not been charged yet.

Monsanto's Bt and RoundUp Ready technologies are failures. Bayer's Bt and LibertyLink technologies are not perceived as failures, yet. Allowing GMO mustard will allow Bayer's LibertyLink into the Indian market. Biosafety assessment aside, this will open the floodgates to herbicide-tolerant varieties of other crops from other companies which, as we all know, are one giant toxic debt-trap for our farmers. Genetically modified crops, by design, will lead to more farmer suicides.

We can no longer call poisons "plant protection products" or "phytosanitary chemicals" or even "medicine" (in Hindi "dawai") because it creates the illusion of safety for humans, and illusion of protection for plants.

Pesticides are poisons.

Pesticides have increased pests, not controlled pests. As a technology, they have failed in their objective.

GMOs as pesticide-producing plants have also failed to control pests and have instead created pests. The case of Bt cotton in India is a clear example.

Ecological science teaches us that pests are created by industrial agriculture through the following processes:

1. Promotion of monocultures;
2. Chemical fertilization of crops — which makes plants more vulnerable to pests;
3. Emergence of resistance in pests by spraying of pesticides; and
4. Killing of friendly species which control pests and disruption of pest-predator balance.

Bt crops are not an alternative to these pest creating systems. They are a continuation of a non-sustainable strategy for pest control, which, instead of controlling pests, creates new pests and super pests. Monsanto advertised that Bt cotton would not need pesticide sprays, clearly a case of false advertising. The primary justification given for the genetic engineering of Bt traits into crops was that Bt will reduce the use of insecticides. A Monsanto brochure showed a picture of a few worms and stated, "You will see these in your cotton and that's O.K. Don't spray." Even today, Monsanto apologists claim that Bt has reduced pesticide usage. The Punjab devastation shows this is not true.

Bt crops are pesticide-producing plants that are supposed to control pests. In the United States, where Bt technology is from, Bt crops are registered as a pesticide.

Bt toxins are a family of related molecules produced, in nature, by a soil Bacterium — *Bacillus thuringiensis* (Bt). Farmers and gardeners have used *Bacillus thuringiensis* in its natural form, as an organic pesticide, for more than fifty years. In recent times, Bt genes have been genetically engineered into crops, making each and every cell in the plant produce toxins through most of its life. Naturally occurring Bt and genetically engineered Bt are not substantially equivalent. The Bt in the soil bacterium is a pro-toxin which is in an inactive state. It is therefore safe for nontarget insects. It is transformed into a toxin by enzymes in the gut of the caterpillar family of insects. In the genetically engineered Bt plant the expression of the toxin does not need this pathway. Bt plants contain an artificial, truncated Bt gene and less processing is required to generate the toxin. It is therefore less selective, and may harm nontarget insects that do not have the enzymes to process the pro-toxin, as well as the pests like the bollworm for which it is intended. This difference in the nature of the Bt in its naturally occurring bacterial form, and its genetically engineered form in plants, is the reason the nontarget species are being impacted while the target species evolve resistance.

The false claim of substantial equivalence by the biotechnology industry has blocked the scientific research that would assess the difference. Science has been supplanted by propaganda.

Genetically engineered Bt crops are being touted as a sustainable pest control strategy while their failure is evident. Bt crops are neither effective nor ecologically sustainable. Instead of controlling pests, Bt crops are creating pests, as is evident from the outbreak of whitefly which destroyed more than 60% of the Bt cotton crop in 2015. Since Bt was introduced in India, pests that had historically never affected non-Bt cotton have become major cotton pests. Massive outbreaks of aphids, jassids, army bugs, and mealy bugs have compelled farmers to use more pesticides than ever before.

There is a global epidemic of non-communicable chronic diseases. According to the World Health Organization (WHO) "Non-communicable diseases (NCDs), such as heart disease, stroke, cancer, chronic respiratory diseases and diabetes, are the leading cause of mortality in the world. This invisible epidemic is an under-appreciated cause of poverty and hinders the economic development of many countries. The burden is growing — the number of people, families and communities afflicted is increasing."[*]

You cannot catch these diseases from other people. You will not get cancer, heart disease or diabetes from sitting next to people with these diseases. The multiple causes are environmental, which means that we can prevent them by changing our habits, food, water etc. to avoid the environmental exposures that cause them.

This book will reveal a large body of published science showing that the pesticide residues in our food are a significant cause of this epidemic and why our children are the most vulnerable to them.

In *Poisoning our Children*, Leu synthesizes the scientific research on the harm caused to public health by poisons and poison-producing plants. He also synthesizes the evidence that farming without poisons is the way of the future.

Poison-free food is the birthright of our children. And we all, collectively, have a duty to protect future generations. André's book is a vital resource for helping us to keep our children safe from harm.

Dr. Vandana Shiva

---

[*] http://www.who.int/gho/ncd/en/

Introduction

Our children are precious, irreplaceable, and our future. This book has been written for parents, as all of us want the best for our children—especially healthy and happy lives.

There is a global epidemic of non-communicable chronic diseases. According to the World Health Organization (WHO) "Non-communicable diseases (NCDs), such as heart disease, stroke, cancer, chronic respiratory diseases and diabetes, are the leading cause of mortality in the world. This invisible epidemic is an under-appreciated cause of poverty and hinders the economic development of many countries. The burden is growing — the number of people, families and communities afflicted is increasing." [*]

You cannot catch these diseases from other people. You will not get cancer, heart disease or diabetes from sitting next to people with these diseases. The multiple causes are environmental, which means that we can prevent them by changing our habits, food, water etc. to avoid the environmental exposures that cause them.

This book will reveal a large body of published science showing that the pesticide residues in our food are a significant cause

---

[*] Source: http://www.who.int/gho/ncd/en/

of this epidemic and why our children are the most vulnerable to them. Unfortunately, most of our children are being exposed to a large range of toxic compounds, because government regulators are not acting on the huge body of scientific evidence linking them to the increase of diseases and behavioral problems affecting children. After more than a century of the average life expectancy increasing, according to many experts, we are now looking at the first generation that will have a lower life expectancy than their parents, a life further complicated by an increase of health problems.[1] Is this the future we want for children?

As mothers and fathers, we must make informed choices regarding our children's health, and to do this wisely we need to be accurately informed. This book examines and clearly explains the risks of synthetic chemicals based on published science. Pesticides will be a primary aspect of this work, as their residues of poisonous chemicals are found in our food, but I will also examine a range of other common chemicals that our children are exposed to and how combinations of even minute amounts of these chemicals and pesticides are responsible for numerous serious diseases.

Most importantly, this book will explain how we can virtually eliminate these risks. There is both good and bad news, but in the end this is a good-news story. We have the option of making simple changes to ensure the best outcome for future generations. As parents, we have a duty to ensure the well-being of our children and their children.

Poisoning Our Children builds on the arguments introduced in my earlier award-winning book, *The Myths of Safe Pesticides** and empowers parents to make informed decisions to ensure the best health outcomes for their children. For those who read my earlier book, the emphasis of this book has changed to focus on children's health. I have kept the same format, based on the five myths, because it is a clear and simple way to inform readers about the major problems with pesticide safety and to ensure consistency with my earlier book. Much of the information in this book is the

---

* Winner in the environment category of the 2014 National Indie Excellence Awards.

same, but I have updated this new book with significantly more data, including many key studies that have been published since the release of *The Myths of Safe Pesticides*. Much has happened in the last few years, most notably the World Health Organization giving glyphosate, the most widespread pesticide used in the world, the second highest rating for causing cancer. Another highly important meta-study was published in a special issue of the scientific journal *Carcinogenesis*, in which over two hundred cancer experts show how mixtures of minute amounts of common chemicals, including pesticides, play a significant role in children developing cancers—both in childhood and as adults later in life.

Consequently, this book is a substantial rewrite, which is why it is being published under a new title rather than as a new edition of *The Myths of Safe Pesticides*.

Scientific research shows that our children are being born pre-polluted by toxic cocktails of pesticides, food additives, and other dangerous chemicals. Numerous scientific studies show that current regulatory systems around the world have failed to protect unborn and growing children from exposure to a massive cocktail of toxic pesticides. A large body of published, peer-reviewed scientific research shows that pesticide exposure in unborn and growing children is linked to:

- Cancers
- Thyroid disorders
- Immune system problems
- Lower IQs
- Attention deficit hyperactivity disorder
- Autism spectrum disorders
- Lack of physical coordination
- Loss of temper—anger management issues
- Bipolar/schizophrenia spectrum of illnesses
- Depression
- Digestive system problems
- Cardiovascular disease
- Reproductive problems (as adults)
- Deformities of the genital-urinary systems

- Changes to metabolic systems, including childhood obesity and diabetes.

Multiple pesticide residues have been found in semen, ovarian follicular fluid, amniotic fluid, maternal blood, placental and umbilical cord blood, breast milk, meconium of newborns, and in the urine of children. The Environmental Working Group found up to 232 chemicals in the placental cord blood of babies.[2]

Children are the most vulnerable to harm caused by chemicals. Young children have the highest levels of pesticide exposure due to their food consumption in relation to body weight. Of particular concern is that the fetus and newborn possess lower concentrations of protective serum proteins than adults, so they cannot detoxify the smallest amounts of toxic chemicals. A major consequence of this vulnerability is a greater susceptibility to cancers and developmental neurotoxicity, where the poison damages the developing nervous system.

Children are also more vulnerable than adults to the effects of endocrine (hormone) disrupters because their tissues and organs rely on balanced hormone signals to ensure that they develop in orderly sequences. Small disruptions in these hormone signals by endocrine-disrupting chemicals can significantly alter how these body parts and metabolic systems develop. These altered effects will not only last a lifetime, they can be passed on to future generations, too. In effect, they program children for a lifetime of ill health.

Most children get the majority of their exposure to pesticides from residues in amounts permitted in food. They get a cocktail of toxic chemicals directly, via their

> **SMALL DISRUPTIONS**
> *in these hormone signals by endocrine-disrupting chemicals can significantly alter how these body parts and metabolic systems develop. These altered effects will not only last a lifetime, but can be passed on to future generations. In effect, they program children for a lifetime of ill health.*

mother's food through the placenta when they are in the womb, or through breast milk. Pesticides used in the house, garden, playgrounds, parks, and sidewalks are other critical areas where children are exposed to pesticide residues. All of these exposure routes have been shown to cause many diseases.

The good news is that they can easily be avoided. Most people are exposed to pesticides through food as well as insect sprays and pest control used in the house and garden. Eliminating pesticides used in the house and garden will make a significant difference; however, the greatest benefits will come from only consuming foods free of pesticides, as the bulk of our exposure comes from foods.

The U.S. President's Cancer Panel report and other research show that around 80 percent of cancers are caused by environmental exposures, especially to toxic chemicals. Eliminating exposure to these, especially for children, as much of the damage is done when they are *in utero* (unborn) or when they are still rapidly growing, is the easiest way to prevent cancer from developing.[3] Preventing cancer and other diseases should be our highest priority, as prevention is always better than cure. No other health initiative can achieve such an impressive reduction in serious diseases, and it is easy to achieve. Now that we know how we can prevent 80 percent of cancers, we should be acting on it now and not waiting for governments to do it on our behalf.

Research shows that eating organic food can virtually eliminate harmful pesticide exposure in a few days. Not only will this prevent the multiple health problems caused by pesticides, but the most comprehensive study ever done comparing organic and conventional foods clearly shows that organic foods are more nutritious and healthy.[4]

The majority of studies show that organic foods have significantly higher levels of disease-preventing antioxidants, so not only does eating organic food significantly eliminate the major causes of multiple diseases, the higher levels of antioxidants protect us and our children from developing them. The question is, how much is your children's health worth? The extra cost of organic food is worth every cent and is the cheapest way to avoid a litany of health problems. The true cost of pesticides in our children's food makes conventional food too expensive. How do you measure the costs of products that can give people a lifetime of poor health compared to those that will help them avoid these problems?

We are told by governments and industries that the pesticides in our food are safe and that we should have no concerns about them. This book critically examines these claims, looking at the science and evidence.

Scientific papers are very technical, with specific jargon that takes time to learn, read, and most importantly, to understand. Most people do not have the time this takes, and consequently this important information is kept largely in the domain of specialist experts. As moms and dads we miss out. This book essentially "translates" the heavy technical jargon into clear, easy-to-understand, everyday language so we can make informed decisions.

As well as learning about the multiple dangers that can be caused by the smallest amounts of pesticides, you will learn about the many serious deficiencies in the regulation and testing of the numerous toxic chemicals used in our food supply. This book will show you that much of the criteria used to underpin the current pesticide use patterns are based on out-of-date and flawed assumptions rather than on the latest published science. In reality, these assumptions are a series of mythologies.

1. **The "Rigorously Tested" Myth.** Most pesticide formulations sold on the market are not tested for safety, and there is no specific testing for the unique requirements of unborn, newborn, and developing children.

2. **The "Very Small Amount" Myth.** Even the smallest amounts of chemical residues can be harmful. Many of these chemicals disrupt the endocrine (hormone) system, and children, especially the developing fetus, are the most vulnerable.

3. **The "Breakdown" Myth.** Many pesticides are actually more toxic when they biodegrade.

4. **The "Reliable Regulatory Authority" Myth.** Regulatory authorities are ignoring a large body of peer-reviewed science

showing the harm caused by pesticides and making decisions on data-free assumptions.

5. **The "Pesticides Are Essential to Farming" Myth.** Toxic synthetic pesticides are not needed in farming, as organic farming is capable of producing enough food to feed the world. Most importantly, eating organic food is the most effective way to protect your children from these damaging synthetic chemicals.

The scientific credibility of pesticide regulatory authorities must be seriously questioned when they are approving the use of pesticides on the basis of data-free assumptions and flawed science. As parents, we should be very concerned that government and industry neglect of published, peer-reviewed science is exposing our children to a lifetime of serious health problems due to pesticide residues permitted in our food.

Given that there are thousands of chemical formulations used in the production of our food, this book would be too long if it went into detail about them all. Instead, I chose to highlight some of the most common agricultural chemicals as examples of the range of issues that surround the widespread use of these substances in our food supply and the environment. Many of the examples featured here are from the United States, Europe, and Australia, as these are the regions that I know the best when it comes to pesticide use; however, the issues are similar in other countries, and in many cases far worse.

The word "pesticide" is used in this book as a generic term for the numerous biocides (poisons) that are used in agriculture, such as herbicides, fungicides, and insecticides. This book is focused primarily on the adverse health effects of pesticides on humans, especially children, with many references to their adverse effects on other species as well.

Data on the adverse effects of pesticides on the environment could fill another, even longer book, as they are substantial and pervade every part of our planet. Pesticides are strongly linked to the massive deaths in many species, especially the rapid decline of frogs, birds, and important pollinating insects such as bees. Pesticides and other chemical pollutants are implicated in the collapse of aquatic ecosystems. They are significant factors, along with land clearing, poaching, and climate change, in the greatest extinction event that this planet has ever faced—much bigger than the extinction event that killed off the dinosaurs. This extinction event is called the Anthropocene Mass Extinction. Whereas we have a few theories about why the dinosaurs went extinct, we know the cause of this great extinction event: us.

The damage caused by agricultural chemicals in the environment and human health began to receive attention in the early 1960s when Rachel Carson wrote *Silent Spring*. These chemicals were shown to persist and accumulate in the environment, causing mortality, birth defects, mutations, and diseases in humans and animals. The number and volume of chemicals used on our food and in the environment has increased exponentially since then.

In the 1990s the issue of chemicals disrupting the reproduction and hormone systems of all species, including humans, was brought to the public's attention by books like Theo Colborn, Dianne Dumanoski, and John Peterson Myers's *Our Stolen Future* and Deborah Cadbury's *The Feminization of Nature*. The peer-reviewed science summarized in these books showed that many chemicals, especially agricultural chemicals, were mimicking hormones such as estrogen, causing serious declines in fertility by reducing the quantity and quality of sperm production and damaging the genital urinary systems. They were major contributors to the dramatic rise in cancers of the sexual tissues—breast, endometrial, uterine, ovarian, vaginal, testicular, and prostate cancers.[5] Endocrine disruption is not just affecting human reproduction; it affects nearly all sexually reproducing species, including plants and animals, as the same hormones are the basis of all sexual reproduction.[6]

We can help reverse this massive extinction event by changing agriculture to use agroecological approaches to produce the high yields of quality food that we need to feed a growing population without toxic synthetic chemicals. Millions of organic farmers are already doing this, and by shifting the billions of dollars spent every year on agricultural research away from toxic chemicals and genetically modified organisms (GMOs) to regenerative organic agroecological agriculture, we could easily produce all the healthy, nutritious, and nontoxic food needed to feed the world without destroying any more valuable ecosystems. Good organic systems ensure that biodiversity increases. In fact, research shows that organic farms have the highest level of biodiversity and serve as refuges for endangered species. Organic farming can also help reverse climate change by stripping the main greenhouse gas, CO_2, out of the atmosphere and storing it in the soil as organic matter. All of these benefits are fully explained in chapter 5.

The choices are quite dramatic. Business as usual will see the continuous decline in human and environmental health, leading to more extinctions as well as lower lifespans and increasing health problems for children. A change to regenerative organic agroecological production systems will reverse this process and lead to greater well-being and health.

A lot of people feel overwhelmed by the immensity of the problem and tune out because they do not know how to change it. As consumers, we can be significant change agents for a better future. It is so simple. Stop using pesticides in and around the house, and buy organic food whenever you have the choice. These consumer dollars will drive the change as retailers and farmers change their sales and production to meet this growing demand. We can stop habitat loss, extinctions, and climate change and give all of us a healthy future.

Real positive change has always been driven by people—not by governments. Be part of this change and join the millions who are already doing their part. We owe it to our children and our future.

NOTES

[1] Joseph Mercola, *Effortless Healing: Nine Simple Ways to Sidestep Illness, Shed Excess Weight, and Help Your Body Fix Itself* (New York: Random House, 2015).

[2] "Pollution in Minority Newborns: BPA and other Cord Blood Pollutants," Environmental Working Group, November 23, 2009, http://www.ewg.org/research/minority-cord-blood-report/bpa-and-other-cord-blood-pollutants.

[3] Suzanne H. Reuben, "U.S. President's Cancer Panel 2008–2009 Annual Report; Reducing Environmental Cancer Risk: What We Can Do Now," President's Cancer

Panel, U.S. Department Of Health And Human Services, National Institutes of Health, National Cancer Institute, April 2010.

[4] M. Baranski et al., "Higher Antioxidant Concentrations and Less Cadmium and Pesticide Residues in Organically-Grown Crops: A Systematic Literature Review and Meta-Analyses," *British Journal of Nutrition* 112, no. 5 (September 14, 2014): 794–811.

[5] Deborah Cadbury, *The Feminization of Nature: Our Future at Risk* (Middlesex, England: Penguin Books, 1998); Theo Colborn, Dianne Dumanoski, and John Peterson Myers, *Our Stolen Future: Are We Threatening Our Fertility, Intelligence, and Survival? A Scientific Detective Story* (New York: Dutton, 1996).

[6] Laura N. Vandenberg, Theo Colborn, Tyrone B. Hayes, et al., "Hormones and Endocrine-Disrupting Chemicals: Low-Dose Effects and Nonmonotonic Dose Responses," *Endocrine Reviews* 33, no. 3 (June 2012): 378–455. First published ahead of print March 14, 2012; Åke Bergman, Jerrold J. Heindel, Susan Jobling, et al., eds., *State of the Science of Endocrine Disrupting Chemicals 2012* United Nations Environment Programme and the World Health Organization, 2013.

MYTH 1

"Rigorously Tested"

"All agricultural poisons are scientifically tested to ensure safe use."

In December 2014, the United States Department of Agriculture (USDA) sent out a news release to all the media outlets in the country about the results of its 2013 Pesticide Data Program (PDP). The headline: "Report confirms that U.S. food does not pose a safety concern based on pesticide residues."

The news release contained the following statement from the United States Environmental Protection Agency (EPA): "The newest data from the PDP confirm that pesticide residues in food do not pose a safety concern for Americans. EPA remains committed to a rigorous, science-based, and transparent regulatory program for pesticides that continues to protect people's health and the environment." So according to the EPA and the USDA, parents should have no concerns because the pesticides in food are safe.

Hundreds of peer-reviewed scientific papers by scientists and researchers challenge this assertion. So, let's look at the science to understand why experts have serious concerns about the safety of pesticides.

One of the greatest pesticide myths is that all agricultural poisons are scientifically tested to ensure that they are used safely. According to the United States President's Cancer Panel (USPCP), this is simply not the case: "Only a few hundred of the more than 80,000 chemicals in use in the United States have been tested for safety."[1] The fact is that the overwhelming majority of chemicals used worldwide have not been subjected to testing. Given that according to the USPCP the majority of cancers are caused by environmental exposures, especially to chemicals, this oversight shows a serious level of neglect by regulatory authorities.

The USPCP 2010 report was written by eminent scientists and medical specialists in this field, and it clearly states that environmental toxins, including pesticides, are the main causes of cancers. Published by the U.S. Department of Health and Human Services, the National Institutes of Health, and the National Cancer Institute, the report discusses many critical issues of chemical regulation.

> Nearly 1,400 pesticides have been registered (i.e., approved) by the Environmental Protection Agency (EPA) for agricultural and non-agricultural use. Exposure to these chemicals has been linked to brain/central nervous system (CNS), breast, colon, lung, ovarian (female spouses), pancreatic, kidney, testicular, and stomach cancers, as well as Hodgkin and non-Hodgkin lymphoma, multiple myeloma, and soft tissue sarcoma. Pesticide-exposed farmers, pesticide applicators, crop duster pilots, and manufacturers also have been found to have elevated rates of prostate cancer, melanoma, other skin cancers, and cancer of the lip.
>
> Approximately 40 chemicals classified by the International Agency for Research on Cancer (IARC) as known, probable, or possible human carcinogens, are used in EPA-registered pesticides now on the market.[2]

Pesticides have been subjected to more testing than most chemicals. However, where chemicals, including pesticides, have been subjected to testing, many leading scientists regard it as inadequate to determine whether they are safe for or harmful to humans. The USPCP report states: "Some scientists maintain that current toxicity testing and exposure limit-setting methods fail to accurately represent the nature of human exposure to potentially harmful chemicals."[3]

There are several key areas in particular in which many experts and scientists believe testing has not sufficiently established that the current use of pesticides and other chemicals is safe.

CHEMICAL COCKTAILS IN FOOD AND WATER

Regulatory authorities approve multiple pesticides for a crop on the basis that all of them can be used in normal production. Consequently, a mixture of several different toxic chemical products is applied during the normal course of agricultural production for most foods, including combinations of herbicide products, insecticide products, fungicide products, and synthetic fertilizer compounds. A substantial percentage of foods thus have a cocktail of small amounts of these toxic chemicals that we absorb through food, drink, dust, and the air. According to the USPCP, "Only 23.1 percent of [food] samples had zero pesticide residues detected, 29.5 percent had one residue, and the remainder had two or more."[4] This means that about half the foods in the United States contain a mixture of chemical residues. Pesticide residue surveys in most other countries show similar results. Because people consume a variety of foods, with around 77 percent containing residues of different types of agricultural chemicals, most people's normal dietary habits include consuming a chemical concoction of which they are unaware.

> *"Only 23.1 percent of [food] samples had* **ZERO PESTICIDE RESIDUES DETECTED**, *29.5 percent had one residue, and the remainder had two or more."*

A study by the U.S. Centers for Disease Control and Prevention (CDC) found a cocktail of toxic chemicals in the blood and urine of most Americans tested.[5] In 2009 the Environmental Working Group (EWG) found up to 232 chemicals in the placental cord blood of newborns in the United States.[6] Many of these pollutants have been linked to serious health risks such as cancer and can persist for decades in the environment.

Regulatory authorities assume that because each of the active ingredients in individual commercial products is below the acceptable daily intake (ADI), the cocktail is thus also safe. They do not test these combinations of chemicals—the chemical cocktails that are ingested daily by billions of people—to ensure that they are safe.

The emerging body of evidence demonstrates that many chemical cocktails can act synergistically, meaning that instead of one plus one equaling two, the joint action can exert a toxic, damaging effect that's three, four, five, or even several hundred times higher than the sum of the two effects when the chemicals act separately.

The World Health Organization (WHO) and the United Nations Environment Programme (UNEP) published a comprehensive meta-analysis on endocrine- (hormone-) disrupting chemicals titled *State of the Science of Endocrine Disrupting Chemicals 2012*. Over sixty recognized international experts worked throughout 2012 to contribute to the meta-analysis and ensure that it was an up-to-date compilation of the current scientific knowledge on endocrine disruptors. This meta-study questioned the practice of testing single chemicals in isolation and ignoring the potential dangers posed by a cocktail of chemicals. "When the toxicity of chemicals is evaluated, their effects are usually considered in isolation, with assumptions of 'tolerable' exposures derived from data about one single chemical. These assumptions break down when exposure is to a large number of additional chemicals that also contribute to the effect in question."[7]

The WHO and UNEP study showed that an additive effect occurred when estradiol (a form of the female sex hormone, estrogen) was combined with other chemicals capable of mimicking estrogen. When each chemical was tested individually at low levels they did not produce any observable effect; however, when they were combined they produced considerable adverse effects. According to the study:

> For a long time, the risks associated with these "xenoestrogens" [artificial estrogens] have been dismissed, with the ar-

gument that their potency is too low to make an impact on the actions of estradiol. But it turned out that xenoestrogens, combined in sufficient numbers and at concentrations that on their own do not elicit measureable effects, produced substantial estrogenic effects. . . . When mixed together with estradiol, the presence of these xenoestrogens at low levels even led to a doubling of the effects of the hormone (Rajapakse, Silva & Kortenkamp, 2002).[8]

An excellent example of this additive effect has been documented in a study published in the peer-reviewed scientific journal *Food and Chemical Toxicology* in 2013. The scientists found that glyphosate, the most widely used herbicide in the world, acts as an artificial estrogen (xenoestrogen) at residue levels commonly found in people, and it induces human breast cancer cells to multiply. The scientists found that these low levels of glyphosate caused a five- to thirteenfold increase in the multiplication of estrogen-sensitive breast cancer cells; however, they had no effect on non-estrogen-sensitive breast cancer cells. The majority of human breast cancers are sensitive to estrogen. This means that estrogen and compounds that act as estrogen cause these types of cancers to grow.[9]

This activity occurred at residue levels of glyphosate that are commonly found in the urine of most people and below the current safety levels set by regulators. "Concentrations of glyphosate tested in this study that exhibited estrogenic activity and interfered with normal estrogen signaling were relevant to the range of concentrations that has been reported in environmental conditions and exposed humans. These results indicated that low and environmentally relevant concentrations of glyphosate possessed estrogenic activity."[10] The term "environmentally relevant" means levels of a chemical that are commonly found in the environment, including in humans. Large numbers of people are being exposed to the estrogenic effects of glyphosate.

The scientists found that when these small levels of glyphosate in herbicides were combined with the normal levels of genistein, a phytoestrogen (plant-based xenoestrogen) found in soybeans, the multiplication of the breast cancer cells increased. The researchers concluded, "This study implied that the additive effect of glyphosate and genistein in postmenopausal woman may induce cancer cell growth."[11]

This additive effect is a great concern considering the vast increase in glyphosate-resistant GMO soybean varieties, which are now being widely used in products such as soy milk, tofu, soy sauce, miso, etc. The scientists cited consuming these soybean products as a possible cause of breast cancer. "Furthermore, this study demonstrated the additive estrogenic effects of glyphosate and genistein which implied that the use of glyphosate-contaminated soybean products as dietary supplements may pose a risk of breast cancer because of their potential additive estrogenicity."[12]

A number of other scientific studies also detail the synergistic and/or additive effects of chemical cocktails in which the cocktail causes health problems even though testing each of the chemicals individually deemed that they were safe.

One of the most significant reviews of the effects of mixtures of low-dose chemicals was published in 2015 in a special issue of the peer-reviewed scientific journal *Carcinogenesis*, titled "Assessing the Carcinogenic Potential of Low-Dose Exposures to Chemical Mixtures in the Environment: The Challenge Ahead." International teams of nearly two hundred cancer biologists and toxicologists reviewed more than a thousand studies and concluded that low-dose chemical mixtures were a significant contributor to causing multiple types of cancer. "Our analysis suggests that the cumulative effects of individual (non-carcinogenic) chemicals acting on different pathways, and a variety of related systems, organs, tissues and cells could plausibly conspire to produce carcinogenic synergies."[13]

A study called "Endocrine, Immune and Behavioral Effects of Aldicarb (Carbamate), Atrazine (Triazine) and Nitrate (Fertilizer) Mixtures at Groundwater Concentrations" in the journal *Toxicology and Industrial Health* showed that combinations of low doses of commonly used agricultural chemicals can significantly affect health. In the experiments conducted by Porter et al. at the University of Wisconsin—Madison, mice were given drinking water containing combinations of pesticides, herbicides, and nitrate fertilizer at concentrations currently found in groundwater in the United States. The mice exhibited altered immune, endocrine (hormone), and nervous system functions. The effects were most noticeable when a single herbicide (atrazine) was combined with nitrate fertilizer.[14]

Atrazine is widely used in agricultural industries in conjunction with synthetic fertilizers that add nitrate to the soil. It is also one of the most persistent herbicides, measurable in corn, milk, beef, and many other foods in the United States. "The U.S. Geological Survey's [USGS] national monitoring study found atrazine in rivers and streams, as well as ground-

IN EUROPE ATRAZINE *was found in most water courses and in a significant percentage of rain samples.[16] In 1999, Swiss research demonstrated that some of the rain falling on Europe contained such high levels of pesticides that it would be illegal to supply it as drinking water.[17] Rain over Europe was laced with atrazine, alachlor, 2,4–D, and other common agricultural chemicals sprayed onto crops. A 1999 study of rainfall in Greece found one or more pesticides in 90 percent of 205 samples taken.[18]*

water, in all thirty-six of the river basins that the agency studied. It is also often found in air and rain; USGS found that atrazine was detected in rain at nearly every location tested. Atrazine in air or rain can travel long distances from application sites. In lakes and groundwater, atrazine and its breakdown products are persistent, and can persist for decades."[15]

In Europe, atrazine was found in most water courses and in a significant percentage of rain samples.[16] In 1999, Swiss research demonstrated that some of the rain falling on Europe contained such high levels of pesticides that it would be illegal to supply it as drinking water.[17] Rain over Europe was laced with atrazine, alachlor, 2,4-D, and other common agricultural chemicals sprayed onto crops. A

1999 study of rainfall in Greece found one or more pesticides in 90 percent of 205 samples taken.[18]

The European Union and Switzerland consequently banned atrazine to prevent this widespread pollution, but it is still broadly used in many countries, and in some cases, as in the United States, is one of the most common herbicides.

The research by Porter et al. showed that the influence of pesticide, herbicide, and fertilizer mixtures on the endocrine system may also cause changes in the immune system and affect fetal brain development. Of particular concern was thyroid disruption in humans, which has multiple consequences including effects on brain development, level of irritability, sensitivity to stimuli, ability or motivation to learn, and an altered immune function.

A later experiment in 2002 by Cavieres et al. found that very low levels of a mixture of the common herbicides 2,4-D, Mecoprop, Dicamba, and inert ingredients caused a decrease in the number of embryos and live births in mice at all doses tested. Very significantly, the data showed that even low and very low doses caused these problems.[19]

Research conducted by Laetz et al. and published in *Environmental Health Perspectives* studied the combinations of common pesticides that were found in salmon habitats and found that these combinations could have synergistic effects. There was a greater degree of synergistic effects at higher doses. The scientists found that several combinations of organophosphate pesticides were lethal at concentrations that had been sublethal in single chemical trials. The researchers concluded that current risk assessments used by regulators underestimated the effects of these insecticides when they occurred in combinations.[20]

One of the most concerning studies, by Manikkam et al., found that exposure to a combination of small amounts of common insect repellents, plasticizers, and jet fuel residues during pregnancy can induce permanent changes in the germ line (the first cells that lead to the formation of sperm or egg production cells) of the fetus. The researchers found that these changes are also inherited by future generations.[21]

A similar study investigated short-term exposure of pregnant female rats to a mixture of a fungicide, a pesticide mixture, a plastic mixture, dioxin, and a hydrocarbon at the time when the fetus was starting sex determination of the gonads. The researchers found that the next three generations had an increase in cysts, resembling human polycystic ovarian disease, and a decrease in the ovarian primordial follicle pool size, resembling primary ovarian insufficiency in humans.[22] The researchers also found that the exposure had changed the way certain genes operated and that this change was passed on to future generations, an effect caused by several different classes of chemicals. The scientists stated, "Epigenetic transgenerational inheritance of ovarian disease states was induced by all the

Epigenetics

Epigenetics is the study of environmental factors that cause changes in the way genes express their traits without any changes in the DNA of the genes. Many of these changes are heritable and can be passed onto future generations.

Scientists now understand that the methylation and histone regions around genes are important in controlling the way genes function. These regions can be affected by environmental factors, such as pesticides, and these changes will alter the way the genes express their traits. They can turn genes off and on or act like dimmer switches to alter the levels of gene expression.

Changes in the methylation and histone regions surrounding the genes are called epimutations. The methylation and histone regions of the developing fetus are very susceptible to pesticides, and research shows that small amounts of pesticides and other chemicals can make adverse changes to these regions around genes. Epigenetic changes to the methylation region can be passed on to future generations, and research is showing that many problems like ovarian disease and cancers can be passed onto children, grandchildren and great-grandchildren from the original parent's chemical exposure.

The meta-review of chemical mixtures in the journal *Carcinogenesis* identified the effect of mixtures of low-dose chemicals—including pesticides—on the epigenome, especially in the fetus, and how this is a significant yet largely ignored cause of the changes that can lead to childhood cancers and to cancers later in life as adults. "The term 'epigenetics' refers to covalent modifications of the DNA (methylation of cytosine in 'CpG islands' within regulatory regions of genes) or of the histones. These modifications can control gene expression and the pattern of modifications is altered in many cancers. For instance, hypo-methylation of proto-oncogenes can lead to overexpression, which is undesirable."*

Proto-oncogenes are genes that can potentially promote changes that can lead to cancer. When chemicals cause them to overexpress, it means that they are increasing the factors that can lead to cancer.

---

* William H. Goodson III et al., "Assessing the Carcinogenic Potential of Low-Dose Exposures to Chemical Mixtures in the Environment: The Challenge Ahead," *Carcinogenesis* 36, no. 1 (June 2015): http://carcin. oxfordjournals.org/content/36/Suppl_1/S254.full.

different classes of environmental compounds, suggesting a role of environmental epigenetics in ovarian disease etiology."[23]

TWO NEW ISSUES OF GREAT CONCERN

These studies raised two new and very concerning issues, firstly the health effects that may occur when low-level residues of common pesticides are combined with minute levels of residues of the numerous other types of common chemicals found in the environment and in humans. This is an area that has been largely neglected by the research community and completely ignored by all regulatory authorities, but it is a major concern in the context of multiple U.S. studies. As previously mentioned, studies have found a cocktail of many toxic chemicals in the blood and urine of most Americans and up to 232 chemicals

> **THE FACT THAT THE RESEARCHERS FOUND** *that combinations of chemicals can cause epigenetic changes that are inherited by future generations is a major issue in terms of the lasting and widespread health damage that is most likely being inflicted on human society.*

in the placental cord blood of newborns in the United States.[24] Many of these chemicals, such as mercury and polychlorinated biphenyls, are known to harm brain development and the nervous system. These studies show the inaccuracy of the regulatory authorities' assumption that because each of these chemicals is present at a low level in commercial products they will cause no health issues. This assumption clearly has no basis in evidence-based science. Regulatory authorities should be making their decisions and taking appropriate actions based on scientific evidence, not on data-free assumptions.

Secondly, the fact that the researchers found that combinations of chemicals can cause epigenetic changes that are inherited by future generations is a major issue in terms of the lasting and widespread health damage that is most likely being inflicted on human society. Regulatory authorities should be taking urgent action to prevent this rather than ignoring the danger.

THE COMBINATION OF THE PESTICIDES PRODUCED BY GMO PLANTS WITH HERBICIDES

Another area emerging as a concern is the combination of pesticides produced by GMO plants themselves with the herbicides and other pesticides used in crop production. Pesticide-producing

GMO crops do not eliminate pesticide usage. They may reduce some types of pesticide usage, but studies show an increased usage of pesticides with GMO plants, especially herbicide usage. Charles Benbrook showed that there was a 527 million pound (239 million kilogram) increase in herbicide use in the United States between 1996 and 2011 due to the increase in GMO crops.[25]

Despite assurances that they have been tested for safety, most Bt GMOs have no or minimal testing. The assumption is that because the Bt toxin is regarded as safe for non-target species, the Bt in the GMO produce is also safe. However, there are several published, peer-reviewed scientific studies showing that Bt toxins cause toxic blood disorders, organ damage and inflammatory diseases in the animals that consume it.[26]

A peer-reviewed, published study that researched the combination of the GMO-produced Bt toxin pesticides and Roundup found that they altered the normal life cycle of cells in human organs. The researchers concluded: "In these results, we argue that modified Bt toxins are not inert on nontarget human cells, and that they can present combined side effects with other residues of pesticides specific to GM plants."[27]

Every cell of a Bt GMO plant and its produce contains Bt toxins, so livestock and people are consuming these pesticides. The products of these pesticide-producing plants have been permitted in the diets of people, especially children, without any peer-reviewed, evidenced-based testing to show that they are safe.

A Canadian study published in the scientific journal *Reproductive Toxicology* found pesticide toxins from GMO crops in the blood samples of women and their unborn babies. GMO Bt toxins were found in 93 percent of maternal blood samples and in 80 percent of fetal blood samples. These women were eating the typical Canadian diet.[28]

COMBINATION OF THE PROTECTIVE COMPOUNDS PRODUCED BY PLANTS AND PESTICIDES

Most plants have protective compounds that they use to resist pests, diseases and weeds. Some of these are toxic, but many of them are antioxidants, such as lycopene in tomatoes, resveratrol in grapes and red wine, and anthocyanins in blueberries and other fruits. When these protective antioxidants are consumed by people, we get the protective benefits as well.

But some of these compounds can cause potential adverse effects, like genistein in soybeans. Genistein is a natural, plant-based estrogen compound (phytoestrogen). Generally these compounds rapidly biodegrade and, if eaten in small quantities, cause no long-term problems. However, as stated earlier, additive and synergistic effects can be a risk when combined with small amounts of other compounds that act like estrogen, as with the previously mentioned example of glyphosate and genistein's effect on the multiplication of breast cancer cells.[29]

This study shows the critical and urgent need to understand how the combination of small levels of pesticide residues and protective compounds in plants have the potential to cause or exacerbate life-threatening diseases such as breast cancer.

SINGLE–CHEMICAL TESTING IS INADEQUATE

The ever-increasing body of peer-reviewed science shows that the current methodology of only testing the active ingredient as a single agent and not testing common combinations is flawed and insufficient to determine the safety of chemical exposure in a real-world situation where humans are exposed to daily cocktails of chemicals.

The USPCP clearly states, "In addition, agents are tested singly rather than in combination. Single-agent toxicity testing and reliance on animal testing are inadequate to address the backlog of untested chemicals already in use and the plethora of new chemicals introduced every year."[30] The meta-review in *Carcinogenesis* came to the same conclusion, stating that not testing combinations is a significant lapse in determining the safety of the chemicals that we are commonly exposed to. "Without a way to anticipate the carcinogenicity of complex mixtures, an important gap in capability exists and it creates a significant weakness in current risk assessment practices."[31]

REGISTERED AGRICULTURAL PRODUCTS

The overwhelming majority of registered pesticide products used in agriculture as insecticides, herbicides, and fungicides are formulations of several chemicals. They are mixtures composed of one or more chemicals that are defined as the active ingredient(s) or active principle and are combined with other mostly toxic chemicals, such as solvents, adjuvants, and surfactants, that are defined as inerts.

The active ingredient is the primary chemical that acts as the pesticide. The other chemicals in the mixture are called inerts because they have a secondary role in the formulation. The name "inert" is misleading as most of these other compounds are chemically active in their functions in the pesticide formulations. They help to make the active ingredient work more effectively. According to the USPCP report, many of these "inert" ingredients are toxic; however, they are not tested for their potential to cause health problems. "Many of the solvents, fillers, and other chemicals listed as inert ingredients on pesticide labels also are toxic, but are not required to be tested for their potential to cause chronic diseases such as cancer."[32]

> *"What the pesticide industry defines as 'inert' ingredients are, in most cases,* **VERY TOXIC MATERIALS INDEED**. *They can include poisons such as acetone, benzene, chlorobenzene, chloroform, ethylene oxide, formaldehyde, formic acid, methyl alcohol, naphthalene, ethylene thiourea and petroleum distillates."*

According to E. G. Vallianatos, in his book *Poison Spring: The Secret History of Pollution and the EPA*, there are around 1,800 inert ingredients in pesticide formulations, and they can account for 99 percent of the volume of products. "What the pesticide industry defines as 'inert' ingredients are, in most cases, very toxic materials indeed. They can include poisons such as acetone, benzene, chlorobenzene, chloroform, ethylene oxide, formaldehyde, formic acid, methyl alcohol, naphthalene, ethylene thiourea and petroleum distillates."[33]

Take for example Roundup and other glyphosate-based herbicide formulations. These pesticides are a mixture of glyphosate as the active ingredient and inerts such as ammonium sulfate, benzisothiazolone, glycerine, isobutane, isopropylamine, polyethoxylated alkylamines, polyethoxylated tallowamine POE-15, and sorbic acid.[34] Glyphosate barely works as an herbicide without the assistance of the inerts to boost its effectiveness.

The active ingredient, glyphosate in this case, is the only chemical in the formulation that is tested for some of the known health problems caused by chemicals—such as cancer, organ damage, birth defects, and cell mutations—to determine a safe level for the acceptable daily intake (ADI) and the maximum residue limit (MRL). The complete pesticide formulation of the active ingredient and the "inerts" is not tested for health problems.

Vallianatos mentions that nearly all pesticide formulations contain petroleum distillates, many of which are carcinogens. This means that the vast majority of pesticide formulations could cause cancer, but to the best of my knowledge not one formulation has been tested by regulatory authorities to see if it causes cancer.

Vallianatos also brings up the synergists that are added to pesticide formulations to strengthen the effect of the active ingredient. "They work by fouling the microsomal enzymes of the liver, which if left alone, would break down highly toxic compounds into harmless molecules. But a pesticide with a synergist is like a killer with a machine gun rather than a pistol."

An example of a common synergist is piperonyl butoxide. It is used in most pyrethroid insecticide formulations to substantially increase the efficacy and toxicity. It works by interfering with the cytochrome P450 group of metabolic enzymes. These enzymes have numerous functions, but one of their most important is to metabolize and neutralize toxins in the body. Piperonyl butoxide interferes with these enzymes, stopping them from breaking down small amounts of pesticide residues, so that the pesticides continue to damage the health of people, animals, and insects. Piperonyl butoxide is very residual, and it is regularly found in food pesticide residue surveys. People are constantly absorbing it through their food, making them and especially children more vulnerable to damage from toxic compounds such as pesticides.

Synergists make the active ingredient kill more effectively—i.e., significantly more toxic—and yet these formulations are not tested under the assumption that their addition will not change the toxicity of the active ingredient. This assumption is clearly unscientific and illogical. How can a synergist be added to make a product more toxic, yet cause no change in toxicity? The credibility and competence of regulators who make these assumptions has to be seriously questioned.

ACUTE TOXICITY AND LD$_{50}$

There are a limited number of registered products in which the whole formulation is tested for acute toxicity, or the amount of the product that is fatal to animals and humans. The most referenced value in acute toxicity tests is LD$_{50}$, which stands for lethal dose (LD) 50 percent, or median lethal dose. This number represents the milligrams of the chemical per kilogram of body mass needed to kill 50 percent of the test animals. The lower the number, the more toxic the chemical because a smaller amount is needed to kill the animals. LD$_{50}$ 100 milligrams per kilogram is more toxic than LD$_{50}$ 400 milligrams per kilogram because only a quarter of the amount is needed to kill the same number of animals.

LD$_{50}$s are widely used as the main reference when judging a substance's acute toxicity, or the adverse effects resulting from either a single exposure or multiple exposures in a short span of time. Adverse effects must occur within two weeks of the chemical being administered to be considered in acute toxicity. LD$_{50}$s are thus irrelevant in showing the longer-term toxic effects of a chemical or compound.[35] These are the toxicities that cause other health issues such as cancers, cell mutations, endocrine disruption, birth defects, organ and tissue damage, nervous system damage, behavior changes, epigenetic damage, and immune system damage. Dr. Kate Short explains this very well in her book *Quick Poison, Slow Poison*, in which the LD$_{50}$s are measurements of the "quick poison," but in reality the main issue with most pesticides is the "slow poison" effect.

Exposure to small amounts of the pesticide can lead to numerous diseases and adverse health outcomes.[36]

ASBESTOS: AN EXAMPLE OF IGNORING THE WARNINGS OF SCIENCE

Asbestos is a good example of how measuring only the LD_{50} can be misleading about a chemical or compound's toxicity. Asbestos does not have an LD_{50} because it is not acutely toxic. It is not a poison in the traditional sense. It is technically possible to eat asbestos by the bucket load and not be poisoned. However, a minute speck of asbestos dust entering the lungs can result in three fatal diseases: asbestosis, lung cancer, and mesothelioma. As early as the 1920s and 1930s there were studies linking asbestos to health problems. Asbestos is a classic case of regulatory neglect and industries misrepresenting the dangers of their products.

The fact that asbestos is not toxic under the LD_{50} criteria was used by the asbestos industry and government regulators for decades to deny that it was a dangerous product, resulting in the widespread and irresponsible use of asbestos in houses, schools, offices, cars, boats, hairdryers, and numerous other applications. Most communities are sitting on ticking time bombs health-wise, with thousands of people in many countries dying from asbestos-related illnesses. Let's compare deaths from asbestos with fatalities from road accidents. In the UK in 2013, 3,002 people died from mesothelioma and asbestosis. According to the UK Health and Safety Executive, when deaths from asbestos-related lung cancer are also factored in, the number of deaths from asbestos diseases in 2013 was around 5,000 people.[37]

In the same year, 1,713 people were killed in reported road traffic accidents in the UK. Deaths from asbestos more than doubled deaths from road accidents, yet asbestos-related

DEATHS FROM ASBESTOS *more than doubled deaths from road accidents, yet asbestos-related illnesses are not getting the same level of attention or funding as programs to reduce road fatalities.*

illnesses are not getting the same level of attention or funding as programs to reduce road fatalities.[38]

The huge costs of removing and disposing of asbestos into toxic waste dumps falls on taxpayers and communities rather than the companies that profited from mining and selling it. Many of these companies deliberately closed down and went out of business to avoid litigation that would cost them hundreds of millions of dollars in penalties.

It took decades of activism by concerned scientists, nongovernmental organizations, and consumers before some regulatory authorities took action to ban or restrict asbestos. However, it is still not banned in most countries, including the United States and Canada. In the meantime hundreds of thousands of people died unnecessary, cruel deaths, and many hundreds of thousands more are yet to die this way because of the twenty- to forty-year latency period for asbestos-related diseases.

Consumers and industries alike should consider the tragedies of asbestos a warning about regulatory neglect of published science.

SCIENTIFICALLY UNSOUND METHODOLOGY

Many scientists and researchers consider it scientifically unsound to test just one component of a mixture and assume that the whole combination of chemicals in a formulation will respond in the same way. Both the U.S. EPA and European Food Safety Authority (EFSA) have testing methodologies for the combined exposure for multiple chemicals, however to the best of my knowledge, these are not used. Instead both, like all regulators, actually reject studies that have more than one chemical because they regard them as confounding their conclusions.

An example of this is the review by the WHO's IARC that classified the herbicide 2,4-D as a possible carcinogen. The IARC review states, "Due to the potential for confounding, studies involving exposure to mixed herbicides or to herbicides containing dioxin were regarded as uninformative about the carcinogenicity of 2,4-D." Consequently, they dismissed these studies and did not consider them even though they showed cancer in humans.[39]

One of the great concerns over this risk assessment process is the dismissal of the studies of 2,4-D that contain dioxins and just using the studies that are based on pure, laboratory-grade 2,4-D. The pure, laboratory-grade standard of most chemicals does not contain the usual impurities that result from the normal commercial production of the chemical. The commercial 2,4-D formulations used in farming contain dioxins, including TCDD, which is regarded as one of the most toxic molecules known to humans. Dioxins are human carcinogens that have no safe level. Vallianatos states: "TCDD initiates and promotes cancer at a potency 17 million times greater than that of benzene, 5 million times greater than carbon tetrachloride, and a hundred thousand times greater than PCBs. TCCD bioaccumulates in animals at dramatic rates: twenty thousand times greater than benzene, six thousand times greater than carbon tetrachloride, and four times greater than PCBs."[40]

Mesnage et al. 2015 found residues of TCDD in commercial animals' feeds. These feeds come from the same crops used to feed humans, so it is reasonable to assume that people eating food from farming systems that use 2,4-D and other chlorinated pesticides are being exposed to levels of TCDD and other dioxins that can cause cancer. Just testing and reviewing the pure active ingredient and not the actual products used in food production that contain toxic impurities such as dioxins gives a false assessment of the actual exposure to toxins and real potential for ill health that they can cause.[41]

Despite the limited testing, there are some studies that compare the differences in toxicity between the active ingredient and the registered formulated product. Glyphosate-based herbicides are amongst the most studied for these effects.

There are numerous studies that show that Roundup is more toxic than its active ingredient, glyphosate. These studies link the pesticide to a range of health problems such as cancer, placental cell damage, miscarriages, stillbirths, endocrine disruption, and damage to various organs such as the kidney and liver.[42]

Research by scientists in France has shown that one of the "inert" adjuvants in Roundup, the polyethoxylated tallowamine POE-15, is considerably more toxic to human cells than the "active" ingredient glyphosate. The researchers found that at one and three parts per million (ppm), doses that are considered to be normal environmental and occupational exposures, POE-15 enters human cells and causes them to die. This is a different mode of action from glyphosate, which is known to promote endocrine- (hormone-) disrupting effects after entering cells. The scientists stated, "Altogether, these results challenge the establishment of guidance values such as the acceptable daily intake of glyphosate, when these are mostly based on a long-term in vivo test of glyphosate alone. Since pesticides are always used with adjuvants that could change their toxicity, the necessity to assess their whole formulations as mixtures becomes obvious. This challenges the concept of active principle of pesticides for non-target species."[43]

RESEARCH SHOWS

that adjuvants used in pesticides can amplify the toxicity of their active ingredient up to 1000 times.

In the only study where nine formulated pesticides were tested on human cells at levels well below agricultural dilutions, the research scientists found that eight of the nine formulations were several hundred times more toxic than their respective active ingredients. The researchers stated, "Adjuvants in pesticides are generally declared as inerts, and for this reason they are not tested in long-term regulatory experiments. It is thus very surprising that they amplify up to 1,000 times the toxicity of their AI [active ingredient] in 100% of the cases where they are indicated to be present by the manufacturer."[44]

Fungicides were the most toxic to human cells, even at concentrations three hundred to six hundred times lower than agricultural dilutions, followed by herbicides and then insecticides. Roundup was the most toxic of the herbicides and insecticides they tested. The scientists concluded, "Our results challenge the relevance of the Acceptable Daily Intake for pesticides because this norm is calculated from the toxicity of the active principle alone."[45]

None of the formulated registered pesticide products are tested for the numerous types of health problems that can be caused by chemicals. ADIs and MRLs are not set for any of these formulated products. They are only set for the "active" ingredient.

It should be of great concern to everyone that the vast majority of the nearly 1,400 registered pesticide and veterinary products used in the United States, around 7,000 used in Australia, and the countless thousands used worldwide for the production of food have had no testing for numerous health and environmental problems linked to the exposure to cocktails of chemicals.[46] All countries share this practice, other than European Union countries, which have started a process of assessing over 143,000 chemicals and chemical formulations.[47]

Given the body of scientific data linking the additive and synergistic effects of chemical mixtures to numerous adverse health effects, serious concerns need to be raised as to why regulators allow these formulated mixtures to be used on the assumption that they are safe. There are no credible scientific data to determine a safety level for the residues of the actual registered pesticide products used in food production and found in food until whole formulations are tested.

QUESTIONING THE CREDIBILITY OF ALL ANIMAL FEEDING STUDIES

A 2015 study by French scientists, published in the scientific journal *PLoS ONE*, calls into question the whole basis of the animal testing models used to determine the safety of pesticides. The researchers analyzed the feed rations used in this testing and found multiple pesticides, heavy metals, dioxins, and PCBs. Pesticides were found in all the samples, with some containing residues of six different pesticides. The majority of these pesticides were organophosphates, followed by glyphosate and AMPA, its primary metabolite.[48]

When researchers are looking for adverse outcomes of pesticide use such as mortality, cancers, birth defects, organ damage etc., the number of these outcomes in the group treated with the pesticide was compared with controls that were not treated with the pesticide. For instance, if the rate of cancer in the controls is similar to the rate of cancer in the groups that are treated with the pesticide, then the researchers will say that there is no statistical difference and the cancer could not have been caused by the pesticide as the group that did not have pesticides had the same level of cancers.

However, it now turns out that these controls were not free of pesticides; in fact, they were exposed to a cocktail of pesticides and other toxic compounds.

> Among other pesticides measured, chlorpyriphos-methyl is an endocrine disruptor and induces anti-androgenic effects and hypothyroidism from prenatal exposure. The presence of these residues could also explain the high levels of mammary or pituitary tumors in rat control populations. Pesticides like malathion, or chlorpyrifos for instance, induce changes in the rat mammary gland. Glyphosate induces human breast cancer cells growth through estrogenic pathways at levels as low as 0.1 ppb, as does Roundup at a comparable level for mammary adenomas growth in vivo. Glyphosate is described as a tumor promoter.[49]

Given the scientific evidence showing the adverse health effects of these cocktails, the scientific validity of these comparison studies has to be seriously questioned. If a substantial proportion of mortality and diseases are caused by toxic contaminants in feed, it makes it very difficult to find a control group that is truly free of pesticides. The results showing similar rates of cancers in the test and control groups indicate not the benign nature of the pesticide tested but rather the ubiquity of toxic chemicals in the environment.

Unless the experiments can compare animals fed pesticide free rations with those dosed with the pesticide, all animal trials showing no difference in adverse health effects between the controls and the treated group have no validity. How can there be a valid scientific comparison when both groups are being fed pesticides?

THE SPECIAL NEEDS OF THE DEVELOPING
FETUS AND NEWBORN

The USPCP and many scientific researchers have expressed concern that the current toxicology testing methodologies are grossly inadequate for children.

The USPCP report stated, "They [children] are at special risk due to their smaller body mass and rapid physical development, both of which magnify their vulnerability to known or suspected carcinogens, including radiation."[50]

This is a critically important issue given that, according to the USPCP, "Approximately 40 chemicals classified by the International Agency for Research on Cancer (IARC) as known, probable, or possible human carcinogens, are used in EPA-registered pesticides now on the market."[51]

The American Academy of Pediatrics published a paper in 2011 titled "Policy Statement—Chemical-Management Policy: Prioritizing Children's Health" that was highly critical of the EPA and its administration of the Toxic Substance Control Act (TSCA) passed in 1976. The paper stated, "It is widely recognized to have been ineffective in protecting children, pregnant women, and the general population from hazardous chemicals in the market-place. It does not take into account the special vulnerabilities of children in attempting to protect the population from chemical hazards."[52]

The main food regulator in Australia and New Zealand, Food Standards Australia and New Zealand (FSANZ), acknowledged in its 20th Australian Total Diet Survey that children had the highest levels of dietary exposure to pesticides due to their size and weight ratios in relation to the amount of residues they receive from food. "In general, the dietary exposure to pesticide residues was highest for the toddler age group. This is due to the high food consumption relative to body weight."[53] FSANZ, along with most regulators, are not concerned about this because pesticide residues in food are usually below the maximum residue limits. However, the USPCP and other scientific researchers have pointed out that the current testing protocols are based on testing mature animals and ignore the specific physiological differences between mature animals and the fetus, newborns, and developing young, including humans.

According to the USPCP, "Chemicals typically are administered when laboratory animals are in their adolescence, a methodology that fails to assess the impact of in utero, childhood, and lifelong exposures."[54]

This is a critical issue as there is a large body of published science showing that the fetus and the newborn are continuously exposed to numerous chemicals. The USPCP stated, "Some of these chemicals are found in maternal blood, placental tissue, and breast milk samples from pregnant women and mothers who recently gave birth. These findings indicate that chemical contaminants are being passed on to the next generation, both prenatally and during breastfeeding."[55]

The U.S. President's Cancer Panel not only expressed concern on the level of these chemical contaminants, they also pointed out that this issue is being ignored by regulators due to the critical lack of knowledge and researchers. "Numerous environmental contaminants can cross the placental barrier; to a disturbing extent, babies are born 'pre-polluted.' Children also can be harmed by genetic or other damage resulting from environmental exposures sustained by the mother (and in some cases, the father). There is a critical lack of knowledge and appreciation of environmental threats to children's health and a severe shortage of researchers and clinicians trained in children's environmental health."[56]

> **THE U.S. PRESIDENT'S CANCER PANEL**
> *not only expressed concern on the level of these chemical contaminants, they also pointed out that this issue is being ignored by regulators due to the critical lack of knowledge and researchers.*

Dr. Theo Colborn, one of the world's acknowledged leading experts on endocrine-disrupting chemicals and coauthor of *Our Stolen Future*, published a peer-reviewed study in the scientific journal *Environmental Health Perspectives* that examined these issues. The study reviewed many of the scientific papers and showed the widespread extent to which children and the unborn are exposed to numerous pesticides. Multiple pesticide residues have been found in semen, ovarian follicular fluid, amniotic fluid, maternal blood, placental and umbilical cord blood, breast milk, meconium (the first feces) of newborns, and in the urine of children. She writes, "It is fairly safe to say that every child conceived today in the Northern Hemisphere is exposed to pesticides from conception throughout gestation and lactation regardless of where it is born."[57]

One of the most comprehensive books on the effects of pesticides on children is *Poisoning Our Future: Children and Pesticides*, by Dr. Meriel Watts. Watts cites numerous studies showing the alarming number of pesticides that can be found in human breast milk and in the placenta. This information is critical as abundant studies show that because children do not have the same protective compounds as adults to metabolize these toxic compounds, even the smallest doses can have a range of profound and negative effects on their health that can affect them their entire lives. Many of these health problems can manifest when they become adults as cancer, reproductive problems, degenerative diseases, and numerous other problems.[58]

CHILDREN'S CANCER RATES ARE INCREASING

A number of studies show the link between chemical exposure, particularly to pesticides, and the increase of cancer in children. The USPCP report states, "Cancer incidence in U.S. children under 20 years of age has increased. . . . Leukemia rates are consistently elevated among children who grow up on farms, among children whose parents used pesticides in the home or garden, and among children of pesticide applicators."[59]

In her book, Dr. Watts cites studies showing that children's cancer rates are increasing globally. They have increased by 35 percent in Britain between 1962 and 1998 and by over 20 percent in fifteen European countries between 1978 and 1997. Many studies she mentions link exposure to pesticides to the increase in many cancers in children and young adults.[60]

The IARC recently classified glyphosate and malathion, two commonly used pesticides, as the second highest level of carcinogens. The classification of 2A—probably carcinogenic to humans—means that they cause cancer in animals and a limited number of studies show that they cause cancer in humans.[61] Malathion (maldison) is still approved as a head lice treatment for children. Given that there are numerous safe alternatives, it is time that it was banned.

Most government surveys do not test for glyphosate, consequently concerned scientists, citizens and civil society organizations are having to test for glyphosate in the environment, in food, and in people's bodies. Testing is starting to show that glyphosate is ubiquitous in all these areas. It has been found to contaminate most watercourses including drinking water, the tissues of most livestock used for human food and in many foods including bread, breakfast cereals, beer, honey, meat, dairy products, vegetables, eggs and fruit. It has been found in the urine of the majority of people tested, showing that most of us are exposed to this highly dangerous pesticide.

The greatest concern is that the testing done by Moms Across America and by Greenpeace in Germany found glyphosate in human breast milk and infant formulas. Mothers are accidently feeding a carcinogen and endocrine disrupter to their children when they are the most vulnerable to the adverse effects of these poisons.*

Because glyphosate is an endocrine disruptor, this means that it has no safety thresholds for use and that the current ADIs and MRLs are meaningless (see chapters 2 and 4 for more details on endocrine disruption, cancer and the multiple diseases linked to glyphosate). Glyphosate is becoming the new DDT in both its scopes of widespread contamination and ability to cause multiple diseases.

NERVOUS SYSTEM DAMAGE

Many pesticides work as nerve poisons. These include organophosphates, synthetic pyrethroids, neonicotinoids, and carbamates. Organophosphates were first developed by German chemists in the 1930s looking to use them as pesticides. They were further de-

---

* http://detoxproject.org/glyphosate-in-food-water/

veloped by the Nazis as nerve gases for warfare in World War II, although it is doubtful they were ever used then. One of the best known organophosphate nerve gases is sarin, which was used to kill thirteen people and injure nearly a thousand in the Tokyo subway attack by the Aum Shinrikyo religious sect on March 20, 1995. Saddam Hussein used a range of organophosphate nerve gases such as sarin and VX gas during the Iran-Iraq War to kill Iranian soldiers and on his own citizens, killing thousands of Kurds. The United Nations (UN) has stated that sarin gas was used by the Syrian government in the Damascus suburb of Ghouta in August 2013, killing an estimated 281–1,729 rebel fighters and civilians. The production and stockpiling of chemical weapons, including sarin, was banned in 1993 by the UN Chemical Weapons Convention. Organophosphates started to become a major class of pesticides after World War II with the commercialization of numerous types such as malathion, parathion, diazinon, chlorpyrifos, azamethiphos, dichlorvos, phosmet, fenitrothion, fenthion, dimethoate, omethoate, tetrachlorvinphos, etc.

Organophosphates react with and destroy a key nervous system enzyme called acetylcholinesterase. This enzyme is responsible for degrading acetylcholine, one of the neurotransmitter chemicals that fire nerve signals like bullets fired from a gun. Acetylcholine is found mostly in the muscle nerves and in the brain. Without acetylcholinesterase to "turn off" acetylcholine, the nerves continue to fire signals, causing a range of symptoms such as intense headaches, nausea, vomiting, muscular paralysis, convulsions, and bronchial constriction. High levels of exposure can cause death from asphyxiation. Low levels of exposure are usually associated with "flu-like" symptoms—headaches, low energy, depression, and a general feeling of being unwell.

Standard toxicology usually regards the reactive degradation of acetylcholinesterase as the only way organophosphates poison animals and posits that they do not damage other metabolic pathways or body organs. Acetylcholinesterase levels will generally recover after low-level exposures, so it is assumed that no permanent damage results from such contact.

There are studies showing that organophosphate pesticides damage other tissues, including the myelin (the protective covering of nerve cells), and key nerves such as the optic nerve, causing permanent damage to eyesight, including blindness. Other studies show genetic damage to the cell chromosomes. This is usually regarded as a sign of a precancerous condition.[62] Malathion, an organophosphate that is widely used in food production, head lice treatment and household bug sprays, has now been given second highest cancer rating by the World Health Organization because it causes cancers in animals.

Dr. Colborn reviewed numerous published papers on one of the most common organophosphates, chlorpyrifos (CPF). These papers detailed an amazing litany of diverse mechanisms in the way CPF affected many tissues and the nervous system, raising serious questions about the safety of CPF, other organophosphates, and all pesticides. These effects included damage to several areas of the brain and disruption of the development of the nervous system in the fetus and newborn that resulted in a range of behavioral problems later in life. She states, "Most astounding is the fact that a large part of CPF's toxicity is not the result of cholinesterase inhibition, but of other newly discovered mechanisms that alter the development and function of a number of regions of the brain and CNS [central nervous system]."[63]

DEVELOPMENTAL NEUROTOXICITY

Scientific research shows that many pesticides affect the normal development of the nervous system in fetuses and children. The brain is the largest collection of nerve cells, and there are several scientific studies showing that when the fetus and the newborn are exposed to minute amounts of these pesticides, even below the current limits set by regulatory authorities, brain function can be significantly altered.

Qiao et al. of the Department of Pharmacology and Cancer Biology at the Duke University Medical Center found that the developing fetus and the newborn are particularly vulnerable to pesticides in amounts lower than the levels currently permitted by most regulatory authorities around the world. Their studies showed that the fetus and the newborn possess lower concentrations of the protective serum proteins than adults.[64] A major consequence is developmental neurotoxicity, in which the poison damages the developing nervous system.[65] The scientists stated, "These results indicate that chlorpyrifos and other organophosphates such as diazinon have immediate, direct effects on neural cell replication. . . . In light of the protective effect of serum proteins, the fact that the fetus and newborn possess lower concentrations of these proteins suggests that greater neurotoxic effects may occur at blood levels of chlorpyrifos that are nontoxic to adults."[66] Contact with chemicals at levels below the regulatory limits can thus harm the fetus and breastfeeding children even if the mother shows no side effects from the contact.

One of the most concerning studies on this matter was published in 1998 by Guillette et al. in the peer-reviewed scientific journal *Environmental Health Perspectives*. The researchers compared the drawing abilities of four- and five-year-old Yaqui children in the Sonora region of Mexico. The study compared two groups of children that shared similar diets, genetic backgrounds, and cultural backgrounds. One group lived in the valley and was exposed to the drift of pesticides from the surrounding farms, and the other lived in the foothills where they were not so exposed. Both groups of children were asked to draw pictures of people. The children from the foothills drew pictures consistent with children their age. The children exposed to pesticides could not draw an image or could barely draw an image that represented a person. Most of their drawings resembled the scribbles of much younger children, indicating that pesticide exposure had severely compromised the development of their brain functions.[67]

THE DUKE UNIVERSITY MEDICAL CENTER *found that the developing fetus and the newborn are particularly vulnerable to pesticides in amounts lower than the levels currently permitted by most regulatory authorities around the world.*

PESTICIDE EFFECTS ON CHILDREN

Some examples from Dr. Elizabeth Guillette's study on the effects of pesticides on children. The children from the valley had been exposed to pesticides far more frequently than the children from the foothills, and the difference in the drawings between the two groups is clear. The exercise revealed a correlation between pesticide exposure and impaired development and motor skills.

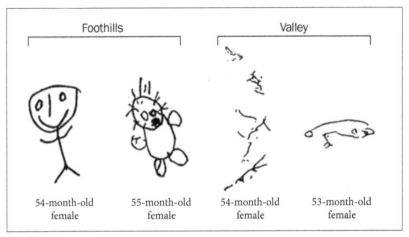

Representative drawings of a person by four-year-old Yaqui children from the valley and foothills of Sonora, Mexico.

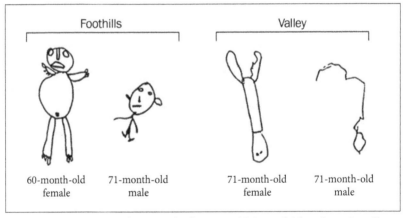

Representative drawings of a person by five-year-old Yaqui children from the valley and foothills of Sonora, Mexico.

Source: Guillette et al., "An Anthropological Approach to the Evaluation of Preschool Children Exposed to Pesticides in Mexico," Environmental Health Perspectives *106, no. 6 (June 1998): 347–53*

ORGANOPHOSPHATES: BRAIN ABNORMALITIES AND IQ REDUCTIONS IN CHILDREN

Concerns raised by Guillette's study about the development of brain function were validated by four later studies that showed that prenatal exposure to organophosphate insecticides (OPs) adversely affects the neurological development of children. The studies were conducted by researchers at the Columbia University Center for Children's Environmental Health, the University of California, Berkeley, and the Mount Sinai School of Medicine. Each study was conducted independently, but they all came up with very similar results: fetal exposure to small amounts of OPs will reduce the IQs of children.

A study of farm worker families in California has shown that by age three and a half, children born to mothers exposed to OP insecticides have lessened attention spans and are more vulnerable to attention deficit hyperactivity disorder (ADHD). Male children were more likely to be impacted.

Parents should have considerable concern that the Columbia University study found no evidence of a lower-limit threshold of exposure to organophosphates in the observed adverse impact on intelligence. This means that even very low levels of exposure could lead to reductions in a child's intelligence.[68]

The study by Rauh et al., published in the journal *Proceedings of the National Academy of Sciences of the United States of America*, has confirmed the findings of the previous studies and shown a large range of brain abnormalities present in children exposed to chlorpyrifos in utero through normal, nonoccupational uses. Exposure to CPF in the womb, even at normal levels, resulted in "significant abnormalities in morphological measures of the cerebral surface associated with higher prenatal CPF exposure" in a sample of forty children between five and eleven years old.[69]

The researchers stated that the current regulatory safety limits and testing methodologies are inadequate for determining safe exposure levels for children.

"Current safety limits are set according to levels needed to achieve inhibition of plasma cholinesterase, a surrogate for inhibi-

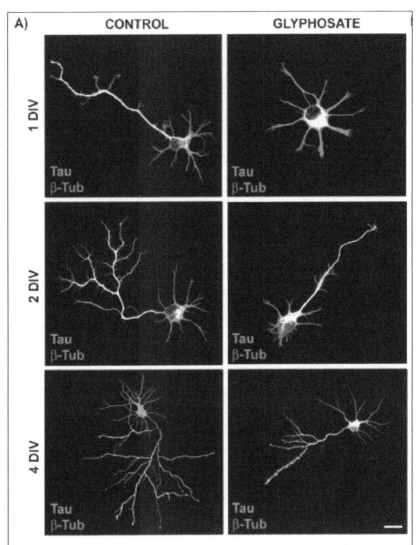

A)

CONTROL | GLYPHOSATE

1 DIV

Tau
β-Tub

Tau
β-Tub

2 DIV

Tau
β-Tub

Tau
β-Tub

4 DIV

Tau
β-Tub

Tau
β-Tub

The glyphosate nerve cells on the right are clearly less developed than the non glyphosate exposed nerve cells on the left. This underdevelopment is of great concern especially in regard to the developing brains of the unborn, new born and growing children.

Source: Romina P. Coullery, María E. Ferrari, Silvana B. Rosso, Neuronal development and axon growth are altered by glyphosate through a WNT non-canonical signaling pathway, NeuroToxicology 52 (2016) 150–161

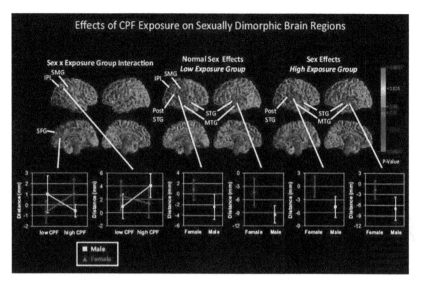

Effects of CPF Exposure on Sexually Dimorphic Brain Regions

The study by Rauh et al., published in the journal *Proceedings of the National Academy of Sciences of the United States of America*, shows a large range of brain abnormalities present in children exposed to chlorpyrifos in utero through normal, non-occupational uses.

Source: Virginia Rauh et al., "Brain Anomalies in Children Exposed Prenatally to a Common Organophosphate Pesticide," Proceedings of the National Academy of Sciences of the United States of America 109, no. 20 (May 2012)

tion of acetylcholinesterase in the brain, long assumed to be the common mechanism by which organophosphates induce neurodevelopmental deficits. However, pathogenic mechanisms other than cholinesterase inhibition are almost certainly contributing to the deleterious effects of early exposure to organophosphates (21, 37), including the observed brain abnormalities and their accompanying cognitive deficits."[70]

Measuring the levels of cholinesterase in blood is the accepted method used to establish the level of exposure to organophosphates. If the levels are considered "normal" then it is assumed that there is no damage to the developing nervous system and the brain. The researchers state that the current assumption that the degradation of acetylcholinesterase is the only way that organophosphates affect the nervous system is incorrect. The abnormalities that the researchers found in the developing brains of children along with the cognitive deficits show that organophosphates have other mechanisms that cause damage.

The researchers recommended that the current limits set by regulatory authorities be revised based on these data. "Human exposure limits based on the detection of cholinesterase inhibition may therefore be insufficient to protect brain development in exposed children."[71]

The United States had banned all uses of chlorpyrifos on food and restricted it to non-food uses prior to these studies. Despite this effort, the exposure levels continue to cause neurodevelopmental problems in U.S. children. The U.S. EPA is now reviewing all uses of chlorpyrifos.

This study has even greater implications for the many countries that allow the use of chlorpyrifos in food crops, especially in the horticulture sector. It is one of the pesticides that are regularly detected in residue surveys of food. Children of these countries almost certainly have had a higher level of exposure to chlorpyrifos.

Another study published in *Environmental Health Perspectives* looked at a range of chemicals, including organophosphate pesticides, that were implicated in lowering the IQs of zero- to five-year-old U.S. children. It found that the reduction in IQ was substantial. The study concluded that "when population impact is considered, the contributions of chemicals to FSIQ [full-scale IQ points] loss in children are substantial, in some cases exceeding those of other recognized risk factors for neurodevelopmental impairment in children. The primary reason for this is the relative ubiquity of exposure."[72]

In a study published in the medical journal *The Lancet Neurology*, scientists from the University of Southern Denmark, the Harvard School of Public Health in Boston, and the Icahn School of Medicine at Mount Sinai, New York, expressed concern that the majority of commercially used chemicals, including pesticides, have not been tested for developmental neurotoxicity. The researchers noted that neurodevelopmental disabilities, including autism, attention-deficit hyperactivity disorder, dyslexia, and other cognitive impairments, affected millions of children worldwide. They stated, "To control the pandemic of developmental neurotoxicity, we propose a global prevention strategy. Untested chemicals should not be presumed to be safe to brain development, and chemicals in existing use and all new chemicals must therefore be tested for developmental neurotoxicity."[73]

A large body of published, peer-reviewed scientific research shows that pesticide exposure in children is linked to:

- Lower IQs
- ADHD
- Autism spectrum disorders
- Lack of physical coordination
- Loss of temper/anger management issues
- Bipolar/schizophrenia spectrum of illnesses
- Depression

The previous studies show that the current methods of determining the MRLs and ADIs for organophosphate and other pesticides are clearly out of date and need to be immediately revised based on the warnings of current, peer-reviewed science. There is an urgent need to investigate the many other biochemical pathways other than acetylcholinesterase that organophosphate and other neurotoxic pesticides can affect.

PYRETHROIDS

Pyrethroids are a group of pesticides based on the chemistry of natural pyrethrum, but they are very different from the natural pesticide. Natural pyrethrum is produced by chrysanthemums and has been used for around 2,000 years as a pesticide in agriculture. The Chinese were the first people to use it by drying and grinding the flowers of chrysanthemums and applying it as a powder onto their crops to kill insects. Two species, *Chrysanthemum cinerariaefolium* and *C. coccineum*, are used for the current commercial production. Like most natural, plant-based pesticides, pyrethrum rapidly biodegrades, leaving no residues in food when used as a pesticide. Sunlight breaks it down in twelve hours, and the normal body temperature of mammals, including humans, breaks it down in four hours. So while highly toxic to cold-blooded animals like insects, it does not have any long-term toxicity for mammals.

The active ingredients in pyrethrum are called pyrethrins. Pyrethrum is a combination of at least six different types of natural pyrethrins that plants change every year as a way of staying one step ahead of insects' ability to develop resistance. Consequently, no insects have developed resistance to pyrethrum, making it one of the most useful pesticides.

Because the natural pyrethrins have low long-term toxicity for humans, the synthetic pyrethroids are promoted as a safe group of pesticides. Nothing could be further from the truth. The synthetic versions of the pesticide have chlorine molecules added to them, causing their chemistry to resemble that of the banned organochlorine group of pesticides. Organochlorine pesticides include DDT, dieldrin, adlrin, heptachlor, and other highly toxic and residual pesticides that have caused and continue to cause a large range of health and environmental problems. They, like pyrethroids, are highly toxic to aquatic species like fish in parts per billion and parts per trillion.

Chlorine was added to synthetic pyrethroids to make them more residual and significantly more toxic. Because natural pyrethrum rapidly biodegrades, it has to be applied often. By making synthetic pyrethroids more residual, they can stay toxic for much longer periods and so do not have to be applied as often. Some pyrethroids can last for years, especially when used indoors for household pest control. Pyrethroids' residues are regularly detected on food, in the environment, and in the blood and urine of people.

Pyrethroids are nerve poisons (neurotoxic) like organophosphates and neonicotinoids. Their mode of action is to keep the sodium channels open, preventing the nerves from turning off after a nerve signal is triggered, which can lead to paralysis and death at higher dosages.

Research has linked exposure to pyrethroids to attention deficit hyperactivity disorder (ADHD), Parkinson's disease, and breast cancer.[74] Richardson et al.'s study, published in the *FASEB Journal*, showed that small amounts of pyrethroids affect the normal development of mice fetuses, causing them to display symptoms of ADHD. Several studies show that pyrethroids are endocrine disruptors.[75] This means that they have no safety thresholds for use and that the current ADIs and MRLs for them are meaningless. (See chapter 2 for more detail on endocrine disruption.)

Piperonyl butoxide is widely used as a synergist in nearly all pyrethroid formulations, including the commercially available natural pyrethrum products. Due to its high level of residual persistence and toxicity, it is prohibited in organic agriculture. Organic farmers who use natural pyrethrum must use the pure form without piperonyl butoxide, which rapidly biodegrades and does not leave residues in food.

RESEARCH HAS LINKED *exposure to pyrethroids to attention deficit hyperactivity disorder (ADHD), Parkinson's disease, and breast cancer.*

Pyrethroids combined with piperonyl butoxide are very common in many household insecticide sprays as well as in head lice treatments. This is one area where children risk high levels of exposure to these toxic and dangerous compounds, and these should be avoided.

However, most people are exposed to pyrethroids from residues in their food. As with all neurotoxic pesticides, parents should make every effort not to feed these to their children directly in their diet or indirectly through the placenta and breast milk.

NEONICOTINOIDS

Neonicotinoids are amongst the newest classes of pesticides. Their chemistry is based on nicotine; however, unlike the nicotine naturally derived from plants, which rapidly biodegrades, these synthetic molecules have been designed by chemists to be more persistent. They can linger for weeks and months as active pesticides, and in some cases they can last for years.

Neonicotinoids have been in the news quite a lot lately as many scientists and researchers are linking them to the global decline in bees and birds. Europe restricted their use in 2013 after investigations by EFSA and independent scientists showed that their risks to bees were unacceptably high. Also in 2013, a study by the American

Bird Conservancy based on two hundred published studies linked neonicotinoids to the dramatic decline of birds in the United States. Neonicotinoids are toxic to a range of wildlife and aquatic species as well as birds and bees.[76]

Neonicotinoids were developed in the 1980s and have rapidly become the most widely used insecticides. Regulators believe they exhibit low toxicity for mammals, including humans, because they bind more strongly to the nicotinic acetylcholine receptors (nAChRs) in insects than mammals. However due to a lack of research their precise effects on the nAChRs in mammals is unknown. [77]

The neurotransmitter acetylcholine activates the nicotinic acetylcholine receptors. As with organophosphate pesticides, high levels of exposure overstimulate the receptors, causing paralysis and death. While organophosphates break down acetylcholinesterase, hindering its ability to degrade acetylcholine in order to terminate nerve signals from these receptors, neonicotinoids bind to the receptors and block acetylcholine from sending signals to the nerves. Acetylcholinesterase cannot break down neonicotinoids, and their binding is irreversible. Nerve signals are blocked until the poison degrades, which in some cases can take weeks and months.

When neonicotinoids biodegrade, their metabolites become more toxic. According to one published study, several of their metabolites and derivatives exhibit high toxicity to mice:

> The excellent selective toxicity of the neonicotinoids is conferred in large part by differential sensitivity for insect versus mammalian nAChRs. However, this observation is based on only the parent insecticide. The selectivity profile of neonicotinoids is not shared with desnitro or descyano metabolites (in animals and/or plants) and derivatives which exhibit high toxicity to mice and high affinity and/or agonist potency to mammalian nAChRs equal to or greater than that of nicotine.[78]

Neonicotinoids persist in the environment. They are largely broken down by sunlight and microorganisms, but without either of these they can last over three years in the environment, causing them to bioaccumulate with regular use.

The USDA Pesticide Data Program in 2006 and 2013 found several different neonicotinoid residues in food, especially imidacloprid (an insecticide). Neonicotinoids now account for around a quarter of all insecticides used in food production, so they are widespread in our food. Research shows that most people have residues of neonicotionoids in their bodies and these come primarily from eating fruits and vegetables. Neonicotinoids are systemic pesticides, meaning that because they are taken up inside the whole of the plant, residues will be inside the grains, leaves, vegetables, and fruits that we eat. Just washing the surface of fruits and vegetables or peeling them will not remove these poisons.[79]

There is very little research into long-term effects of exposure to small amounts of neonicotinoids on humans, especially for the fetus and growing children. Unlike older pesticides such as organochlorines and organophosphates, which have hundreds of studies on their long-term effects on mammals, neonicotinoids seem to be ignored. nAChRs are important for brain function in mammals, especially brain development in the fetus, growing children and teenagers. One published study found that the neonicotinoids, Acetamiprid and Imidacloprifon, exerted similar excitatory effects as nicotine did on mammalian nAChRs. The researchers concluded: "Therefore, the neonicotinoids may adversely affect human health, especially the developing brain." Neonicotinoids and their metabolites can cross the brain blood barrier damaging the brains of mammals, so it is reasonable to assume that the same will occur in humans. [80]

Given the numerous studies showing that the developing fetus, newborn, and children are particularly sensitive to the smallest amounts of toxic chemicals, it is not unreasonable to assume that they are just as sensitive to neonicotinoids. Neonicotinoids are nerve poisons, and based on the numerous studies showing how other nerve poisons such as organophosphates, pyrethroids, heavy metals (lead, mercury, cadmium, etc.), and many other chemicals cause developmental neurotoxicity in children, the lack of testing

HOW CAN THE ADIs *or the MRLs have any validity for children if there is no evidenced-based scientific data to prove that long-term exposure at these levels are safe?*

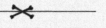

should ring alarm bells. Instead, the effects of neonicotinoids on children are being ignored by regulators and researchers. An absence of information about harm due to lack of research does not mean that a chemical is safe. This is the regulatory equivalent of the ostrich sticking its head in the sand so it won't see the obvious danger.

The greatest evidence of the multiple health problems that neonicotinoids could cause comes from what we learnt about nicotine and the long-term effects of being exposed to it through smoking or chewing tobacco. All neonicotinoids are types of nicotine, but unlike natural nicotine that rapidly biodegrades, these synthetic molecules are persistent and can bioaccumulate so that their effects last longer in the body. Children are being exposed every day to small amounts of these toxic synthetic nicotine derivatives and metabolites through residues in food. Science shows that regular exposure to nicotine through smoking and chewing tobacco, even passively, leads to multiple diseases such as cancers, heart disease, lung disease, etc.

The credibility of regulatory authorities has to be seriously questioned when they are approving a group of pesticides that result in people being exposed to nicotine chemicals everyday, without doing any research into the long-term effects, especially for children. Given the extensive science showing the harm caused by tobacco and neurotoxic pesticides, using data-free assumptions to establish the ADIs or MRLs for neonicotinoids lacks scientific credibility. How can the ADIs or the MRLs have any validity for children if there is no evidenced-based scientific data to prove that long-term exposure at these levels are safe?

DAMAGE PASSED ON TO FUTURE GENERATIONS

Some of the most concerning studies show that pesticide damage can be passed on to the next generation. Not only are the offspring born with damage to the nervous system, the reproductive system, and other organs, the great-grandchildren can be as well.[81]

Researchers in a 2012 study found that pregnant rats and mice exposed to the fungicide vinclozolin during the period when the fetus was developing reproductive organs, developed genetic changes in the genes that were passed on to future generations. The researchers stated, "Transient exposure of the F0 generation* gestating female during gonadal sex determination promoted transgenerational adult onset disease in F3 generation male and female mice, including spermatogenic cell defects, testicular abnormalities, prostate abnormalities, kidney abnormalities and polycystic ovarian disease. Pathology analysis demonstrated 75% of the vinclozolin lineage animals developed disease with 34% having two or more different disease states."[82]

Another study showed that when pregnant rats were exposed to a combination of permethrin, a common pyrethroid insecticide,

---

* F0 is the first generation, F1 their children, F2 their grandchildren, and so on.

NUMBER OF CHILDREN (6–21 YRS) WITH AUTISM SERVED BY IDEA

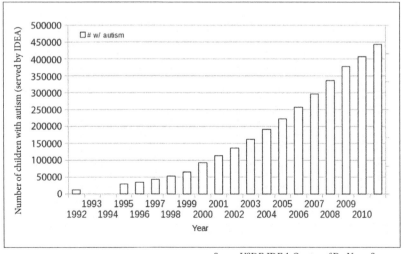

Source: USDE:IDEA, Courtesy of Dr. Nancy Swanson

and DEET (N,N-diethyl-meta-toluamide), the most common insect repellent, significant damage occurred in subsequent generations, including the great-grandchildren. The researchers found that "Gestating F0 generation female rats were exposed during fetal gonadal sex determination and the incidence of disease evaluated in F1 and F3 generations. There were significant increases in the incidence of total diseases in animals from pesticide lineage F1 and F3 generation animals. Pubertal abnormalities, testis disease, and ovarian disease (primordial follicle loss and polycystic ovarian disease) were increased in F3 generation animals."[83]

The significant issue with these two studies is that small exposures to pesticides at critical times in the development of the fetus can cause multiple diseases that are passed on to future generations. It means that pregnant women eating food with minute levels of pesticides could be inadvertently exposing their children, grandchildren, and great-grandchildren to permanent damage to their reproductive systems and other organs.

The scientists found that 363 regions of the epigenome had been altered by the pesticides, "Analysis of the pesticide lineage F3 generation sperm epigenome identified 363 differential DNA methylation regions (DMR) termed epimutations. Observations demonstrate that a pesticide mixture (permethrin and DEET) can promote epigenetic transgenerational inheritance of adult onset disease and potential sperm epigenetic biomarkers for ancestral environmental exposures."[84]

Genes and the whole epigenome play a major role in the development of hormone, metabolic, reproductive, nervous, and other body systems, and in the development of organs, limbs, the brain, and other body parts. When genes and the epigenome are altered, this means that the development of the systems and organs that are dependent on the signals from genes are altered, leading to a range of diseases and other problems later in life.

This study is particularly distressing because DEET is the most common repellent used for mosquitoes and other insects. It is widely used on children and pregnant women. A U.S. study found DEET in 100 percent of cord blood samples.[85]

PUBLISHED, PEER-REVIEWED SCIENCE
IS SUBSTANTIAL AND COMPELLING

Numerous scientific studies show that current regulatory systems around the world have failed to protect unborn and growing children from exposure to a massive cocktail of toxic pesticides and chemicals. The body of published, peer-reviewed science showing the wide range of problems caused by pesticides to the fetus and newborn is substantial and compelling. The current testing methodologies use adolescent through to adult animals. This means that they will not detect the adverse health issues that are specific to the unborn and small children.

Despite the fact that many professional experts in this area such as the USPCP, the WHO, and UNEP and The American Academy of Pediatrics have been calling for specific toxicological studies that are relevant to the fetus and growing children to determine if the current MRLs and ADIs of pesticides are safe for them, regulatory authorities largely continue to ignore this dangerous oversight. Until these specific tests are done, regulatory authorities are using data-free assumptions that the current pesticides used in food, households, playgrounds, schools, and in the general environment are safe for our unborn and growing children. Regulation should not be based on assumptions but should use independently published, peer-reviewed scientific evidence to prove whether these toxins are safe. The evidence shows that it is a myth that all agricultural poisons are rigorously tested to ensure safe use. As parents, we should be seriously concerned about this. Given that our children are our future and most of them are exposed to multiple chemicals, time will prove the regulatory committees' unwillingness to act against pesticides more serious than their decades of inaction over asbestos.

NOTES

[1] "U.S. President's Cancer Panel Annual Report," 2010.

[2] Ibid.

[3] Ibid.

[4] Ibid.

[5] Margo Higgins, "Toxins Are in Most Americans' Blood, Study Finds," *Environmental News Network*, March 26, 2001; "U.S. President's Cancer Panel Annual Report," 2010.

[6] "U.S. President's Cancer Panel Annual Report," 2010.

[7] Bergman et al., *State of the Science of Endocrine Disrupting Chemicals 2012*.

[8] Ibid.

[9] Mohan Manikkam et al., "Transgenerational Actions of Environmental Compounds on Reproductive Disease and Identification of Epigenetic Biomarkers of Ancestral Exposures," *PLoS ONE* 7, no. 2 (February 2012).

[10] Eric Nilsson et al., "Environmentally Induced Epigenetic Transgenerational Inheritance of Ovarian Disease." *PLoS ONE* 7, no. 5 (May 2012): e36129. doi:10.1371/journal.pone.00361.

[11] Ibid.

[12] "U.S. President's Cancer Panel Annual Report," 2010.

[13] William H. Goodson III et al., "Assessing the Carcinogenic Potential of Low-Dose Exposures to Chemical Mixtures in the Environment: The Challenge Ahead," *Carcinogenesis* 36, no. 1 (June 2015): http://carcin.oxfordjournals.org/content/36/Suppl_1/S254.full.

[14] Warren P. Porter, James W. Jaeger, and Ian H. Carlson, "Endocrine, Immune and Behavioral Effects of Aldicarb (Carbamate), Atrazine (Triazine) and Nitrate (Fertilizer) Mixtures at Groundwater Concentrations," *Toxicology and Industrial Health* 15 (January 1999): 133–50.

[15] Caroline Cox, "Atrazine: Environmental Contamination and Ecological Effects," Northwest Coalition against Pesticides, Eugene, Oregon, *Journal of Pesticide Reform* 21, no. 3 (Fall 2001): 12.

[16] Charizopoulos and Papadopoulou-Mourkidou, "Occurrence of Pesticides in Rain of the Axios River Basin, Greece."

[17] "U.S. President's Cancer Panel Annual Report," 2010.

[18] Bergman et al., *State of the Science of Endocrine Disrupting Chemicals 2012*.

[19] María Fernanda Cavieres, James Jaeger, and Warren Porter, "Developmental Toxicity of a Commercial Herbicide Mixture in Mice: I. Effects on Embryo Implantation and Litter Size," *Environmental Health Perspectives* 110, no. 11 (November 2002): 1081–85.

[20] Cathy A. Laetz et al., "The Synergistic Toxicity of Pesticide Mixtures: Implications for Risk Assessment and the Conservation of Endangered Pacific Salmon," *Environmental Health Perspectives* 117, no. 3 (March 2009): 348–53.

[21] Manikkam et al., "Transgenerational Actions of Environmental Compounds."

[22] Eric Nilsson et al., "Environmentally Induced Epigenetic Transgenerational Inheritance of Ovarian Disease." *PLoS ONE* 7, no. 5 (May 2012): e36129. doi:10.1371/journal.pone.00361.

[23] Ibid.

[24] "U.S. President's Cancer Panel Annual Report," 2010.

[25] Charles Benbrook, "Impacts of Genetically Engineered Crops on Pesticide Use in the U.S.—The First Sixteen Years," *Environmental Sciences Europe* 24, no. 24 (September 2012): doi:10.1186/2190-4715-24-24; Jack A. Heinemann et al., "Sustainability and Innovation in Staple Crop Production in the US Midwest," *International Journal of Agricultural Sustainability*, published online June 14, 2013, http://www.tandfonline.com/doi/full/10.1080/14735903.2013.806408#.Ut766dLnaU.

[26] Bélin Poletto Mezzomo, Ana Luisa Miranda-Vilela, Ingrid de Souza Freire, Lilian Carla Pereira Barbosa, Flávia Arruda Portilho, Zulmira Guerrero Marques Lacava, Cesar Koppe Grisolia, "Hematotoxicity of Bacillus thuringiensis as Spore-crystal Strains Cry1Aa, Cry1Ab, Cry1Ac or Cry2Aa in Swiss Albino Mice," *Journal of Hematology & Thromboembolic Diseases* 1: 104 (March 16, 2013).

[27] Robin Mesnage et al., "Cytotoxicity on Human Cells of Cry1Ab and Cry1Ac Bt Insecticidal Toxins Alone or with a Glyphosate-Based Herbicide," *Journal of Applied Toxicology* 33, no. 7 (July 2013): 695–99. Originally published online February 2012.

[28] A. Aris and S. Leblanc, "Maternal and Fetal Exposure to Pesticides Associated to Genetically Modified Foods in Eastern Townships of Quebec, Canada," *Reproductive Toxicology* 31, no. 4 (May 2011): 528–33.

[29] "U.S. President's Cancer Panel Annual Report," 2010.

[30] Ibid.

[31] Goodson et al., "Assessing the Carcinogenic Potential of Low-Dose Exposures to Chemical Mixtures in the Environment."

[32] "U.S. President's Cancer Panel Annual Report," 2010.

[33] E. G. Vallianatos and McKay Jenkins, *Poison Spring: The Secret History of Pollution and the EPA* (New York: Bloomsbury Press, 2014). All quotes from the following four paragraphs are from this source.

[34] Caroline Cox, "Glyphosate (Roundup)," Northwest Coalition against Pesticides, Eugene, Oregon, *Journal of Pesticide Reform* 24, no. 4 (Winter 2004).

[35] Short, *Quick Poison, Slow Poison*.

[36] Ibid.

[37] "Statistics: Asbestos Related Diseases," Health and Safety Executive, UK, 2015, http://www.hse.gov.uk/statistics/causdis/asbestos.htm.

[38] "Transparency Data: Annual Road Fatalities," Department for Transport, UK, June 30, 2011 (last updated September 29, 2014), https://www.gov.uk/government/publications/annual-road-fatalities.

[39] Dana Loomis, et al., "Carcinogenicity of Lindane, DDT, and 2,4-dichlorophenoxyacetic Acid," *Lancet Oncology* 16, no. 8 (June 22, 2015): 891–92.

40 Vallianatos and Jenkins, *Poison Spring*.

41 EPA, "Risk Assessment Guidance for Superfund Volume I Human Health Evaluation Manual (Part A)," December 1989, http://www.epa.gov/sites/production/files/2015-09/documents/rags_a.pdf; EFSA, "International Frameworks Dealing with Human Risk Assessment of Combined Exposure to Multiple Chemicals," *EFSA Journal* 11, no. 3313 (2013); Loomis, "Carcinogenity of Lindane."

42 Cox, "Glyphosate (Roundup)"; Sophi Richard, Safa Moslemi, Herbert Sipahutar, Nora Benachour, and Gilles-Éric Séralini, "Differential Effects of Glyphosate and Roundup on Human Placental Cells and Aromatase," *Environmental Health Perspectives* 113, no. 6 (June 2005): 716–20. Published online February 25, 2005, http://www.ncbi.nlm.nih.gov/pmc/articles/PMC1257596/; Robin Mesnage, Benoît Bernay, and Gilles-Éric Séralini, "Ethoxylated Adjuvants of Glyphosate-Based Herbicides are Active Principles of Human Cell Toxicity," *Toxicology* 313, nos. 2–3 (November 2013): 122–28. Published online September 21, 2012, http://dx.doi.org/10.1016/j.tox.2012.09.006.

43 Mesnage et al., "Ethoxylated Adjuvants of Glyphosate-Based Herbicides."

44 Robin Mesnage et al., "Major Pesticides Are More Toxic to Human Cells than Their Declared Active Principles," *BioMed Research International* (December 2013), http://www.hindawi.com/journals/bmri/aip/179691/.

45 Ibid.

46 "U.S. President's Cancer Panel Annual Report," 2010; Australian Pesticides and Veterinary Medicines Authority (APVMA), "About the APVMA: Factsheet," September 2008, http://www.apvma.gov.au/publications/fact_sheets/docs/about_apvma.pdf.

47 European Commission, "What is REACH?," January 24, 2014, http://ec.europa.eu/environment/chemicals/reach/reach_en.htm.

48 Robin Mesnage et al., "Laboratory Rodent Diets Contain Toxic Levels of Environmental Contaminants: Implications for Regulatory Tests," *PLoS ONE* 10, no. 7 (July 2, 2015): http://www.ncbi.nlm.nih.gov/pmc/articles/PMC4489719/.

49 Ibid.

50 "U.S. President's Cancer Panel Annual Report," 2010.

51 Ibid.

52 "Policy Statement—Chemical-Management Policy: Prioritizing Children's Health," American Academy of Pediatrics, 2011, http://pediatrics.aappublications.org/content/127/5/983.full.pdf.

53 Food Standards Australia and New Zealand, "20th Australian Total Diet Survey," 2002, available online at http://www.foodstandards.gov.au/publications/Pages/20thaustraliantotaldietsurveyjanuary2003/20thaustraliantotaldietsurveyfullreport/Default.aspx.

54 "U.S. President's Cancer Panel Annual Report," 2010.

55 Ibid.

[56] Ibid.

[57] Theo Colborn, "A Case for Revisiting the Safety of Pesticides: A Closer Look at Neurodevelopment," *Environmental Health Perspectives* 114, no. 1 (January 2006): 10–17.

[58] Meriel Watts, *Poisoning Our Future: Children and Pesticides*, Pesticide Action Network Asia and Pacific, 2013.

[59] "U.S. President's Cancer Panel Annual Report," 2010.

[60] Watts, *Poisoning Our Future*.

[61] "Glyphosate," IARC Monographs–112, http://monographs.iarc.fr/ENG/Monographs/vol112/mono112-02.pdf.

[62] Cox, "Glyphosate (Roundup)."

[63] Colborn, "A Case for Revisiting the Safety of Pesticides."

[64] Dan Qiao, Frederic Seidler, and Theodore Slotkin, "Developmental Neurotoxicity of Chlorpyrifos Modeled In Vitro: Comparative Effects of Metabolites and Other Cholinesterase Inhibitors on DNA Synthesis in PC12 and C6 Cells," *Environmental Health Perspectives* 109, no. 9 (September 2001): 909–13.

[65] Justin Aldridge et al., "Serotonergic Systems Targeted by Developmental Exposure to Chlorpyrifos: Effects during Different Critical Periods," *Environmental Health Perspectives* 111, no. 14 (November 2003): 1736–43; Gennady A. Buznikov et al., "An Invertebrate Model of the Developmental Neurotoxicity of Insecticides: Effects of Chlorpyrifos and Dieldrin in Sea Urchin Embryos and Larvae," *Environmental Health Perspectives* 109, no. 7 (July 2001): 651–61; Gertrudis Cabello et al., "A Rat Mammary Tumor Model Induced by the Organophosphorous Pesticides Parathion and Malathion, Possibly through Acetylcholinesterase Inhibition," *Environmental Health Perspectives* 109, no. 5 (May 2001): 471–79.

[66] Qiao, Seidler, and Slotkin, "Developmental Neurotoxicity of Chlorpyrifos Modeled In Vitro."

[67] Elizabeth A. Guillette et al., "An Anthropological Approach to the Evaluation of Preschool Children Exposed to Pesticides in Mexico," *Environmental Health Perspectives* 106, no. 6 (June 1998): 347–53.

[68] Virginia Rauh et al., "Brain Anomalies in Children Exposed Prenatally to a Common Organophosphate Pesticide," *Proceedings of the National Academy of Sciences of the United States of America* 109, no. 20 (May 2012), www.pnas.org/cgi/doi/10.1073/pnas.1203396109; Maryse F. Bouchard et al., "Prenatal Exposure to Organophosphate Pesticides and IQ in 7-Year-Old Children," *Environmental Health Perspectives* 119, no. 8 (August 2011): 1189–95, published online April 21, 2011, http://www.ncbi.nlm.nih.gov/pmc/articles/PMC3237357/; Stephanie M. Engel et al., "Prenatal Exposure to Organophosphates, Paraoxonase 1, and Cognitive Development in Children," *Environmental Health Perspectives* 119 (2011): 1182–88, published online April 21, 2011, http://ehp.niehs.nih.gov/1003183/.

[69] Rauh et al., "Brain Anomalies in Children Exposed Prenatally."

[70] Ibid.

[71] Ibid.

[72] David C. Bellinger, "A Strategy for Comparing the Contributions of Environmental Chemicals and Other Risk Factors to Neurodevelopment of Children," Environmental Health Perspectives 120, no. 4 (2012): 501–7, http://dx.doi.org/10.1289/ehp.1104170.

[73] Philippe Grandjean and Philip J. Landrigan, "Neurobehavioural Effects of Developmental Toxicity," The Lancet Neurology 13, no. 3 (March 2014): 330–38.

[74] J. R. Richardson et al., "Developmental Pesticide Exposure Reproduces Features of Attention Deficit Hyperactivity Disorder," FASEB Journal 29, no. 5 (May 2015):1960–72; M. A. Elwan et al., "Pyrethroid Pesticide-Induced Alterations in Dopamine Transporter Function," Toxicology and Applied Pharmacology 211, no. 3 (March 15, 2006): 188–97; V. Go, J. Garey, M. S. Wolff, and B. G. Pogo, "Estrogenic Potential of Certain Pyrethroid Compounds in the MCF-7 Human Breast Carcinoma Cell Line," Environmental Health Perspectives 107, no. 3 (March 1999): 173–77.

[75] Susanne M. Brander, Guochun He, Kelly L. Smalling, Michael S. Denison, and Gary N. Cherr, "The In Vivo Estrogenic and In Vitro Anti-Estrogenic Activity of Permethrin and Bifenthrin," Environmental Toxicology and Chemistry 31, no. 12 (December 2012): 2848–55.

[76] Pierre Mineau and Cynthia Palmer, "The Impact of the Nation's Most Widely Used Insecticides on Birds," Neonicotinoid Insecticides and Birds, American Bird Conservancy, 2013.

[77] Kimura-Kuroda J, Komuta Y, Kuroda Y, Hayashi M, Kawano H (2012) Nicotine-Like Effects of the Neonicotinoid Insecticides Acetamiprid and Imidaclopridon Cerebellar Neurons from Neonatal Rats. PLoS ONE 7(2): e32432. doi:10.1371/journal.pone.0032432

[78] Motohiro Tomizawa, "Neonicotinoids and Derivatives: Effects in Mammalian Cells and Mice," Journal of Pesticide Science 29, no. 3 (2004): 177–83.

[79] Harada KH, Tanaka K, Sakamoto H, Imanaka M, Niisoe T, Hitomi T, et al. (2016) Biological Monitoring of Human Exposure to Neonicotinoids Using Urine Samples, and Neonicotinoid Excretion Kinetics. PLoS ONE 11(1): e0146335. doi:10.1371/journal.pone.0146335

[80] Kimura-Kuroda J, Komuta Y, Kuroda Y, Hayashi M, Kawano H (2012) Nicotine-Like Effects of the Neonicotinoid Insecticides Acetamiprid and Imidaclopridon Cerebellar Neurons from Neonatal Rats. PLoS ONE 7(2): e32432. doi:10.1371/journal.pone.0032432

[81] Manikkam et al., "Transgenerational Actions of Environmental Compounds on Reproductive Disease; Carlos Guerrero-Bosagna et al., "Epigenetic Transgenerational Inheritance of Vinclozolin Induced Mouse Adult Onset Disease and Associated Sperm Epigenome Biomarkers," Reproductive Toxicology 34, no. 4 (December 2012): 694–

707; Mohan Manikkam et al., "Pesticide and Insect Repellent Mixture Permethrin and DEET Induces Epigenetic Transgenerational Inheritance of Disease and Sperm Epimutations," *Journal of Reproductive Toxicology* 34, no. 4 (December 2012): 708–19.

[82] Guerrero-Bosagna et al., "Epigenetic Transgenerational Inheritance."

[83] Manikkam et al., "Pesticide and Insect Repellent Mixture Permethrin and DEET."

[84] Ibid.

[85] Watts, *Poisoning Our Future.*

MYTH 2

✖

"Very Small Amount"

"The residues are too low to cause any problems."

Most developed nations have pesticide residue programs in which food is periodically tested for pesticide residues exceeding the maximum residue limits (MRLs) and the acceptable daily intake (ADI). This testing shows that the pesticide residues in food are generally below the MRLs and ADIs. It is on the basis of this testing that the regulatory authorities state that the food is safe, as the residues are too low to cause any problems.

There are, however, serious concerns about the way these MRLs and ADIs are set, several of which were explained in the previous chapter.

The growing body of published science on endocrine disruption, in which very small amounts of some types of synthetic chemicals can act like hormones and disrupt our hormone systems, is another area where many scientists are concerned that the current methods of assessing the toxicity of synthetic chemicals in our diet and environment are out of date and grossly inadequate in determining safe levels of exposure.

Dose Responses

Dose responses measure how a particular amount of a substance affects us. See the graphs in this chapter for a visual example of these response curves.

Monotonic dose response: Response decreases as dosage decreases.

Non-linear dose response: Response does not change in direct proportion to dosage amount.

Non-monotonic dose response: Response begins to decrease as dosage decreases, but then begins to increase as dosage continues to decrease.

The 2013 meta-study by the WHO and UNEP clearly states that there are many gaps in the current testing methods used to determine the safety of chemicals, including that the current tests are not able to screen chemicals for hormone-disrupting effects. "Perhaps most importantly, the exposure periods do not cover critical developmental windows of increased susceptibility now known to exist."[1]

As the fetus develops, small levels of hormones at specific times signal genes to develop various body systems such as limbs and the nervous, metabolic, and reproductive systems. These times are known as critical developmental windows of increased susceptibility for children. In many cases these changes only require hormones at very low levels, in parts per billion or parts per trillion, to send the appropriate signal to ensure the normal development of the child. To understand a part per trillion, it is equivalent to adding one drop into more than three Olympic-sized swimming pools. The smallest amounts of many chemicals, including numerous pesticides, can act like hormones and disrupt the normal development of children by interfering with these critical developmental windows of increased susceptibility. Regulatory authorities are largely ignoring this very important issue. Although many countries have passed laws more than a decade ago requiring pesticides to be reviewed for endocrine disruption, so far this hasn't been done.

The current model of toxicology (science of poisons) works on the notion that the lower the dose, the less the effect of the poison. When animal testing shows that a certain dose level of poison causes no observed adverse effects (NOAEL), this dose becomes the basis that is used to determine the ADI. The ADI is usually determined by lowering the permitted amount by a factor of a hundred times lower.

The MRL is derived through a more complex and convoluted process. It is based on the amount of the pesticide needed to control the pest, weed, or disease. This amount is determined through field trials wherein produce is tested to determine the amount of residues it contains. Regulators make an assumption regarding how much of the produce will be consumed daily in the average diet, and as long as the residues on this amount do not exceed the ADI, then the MRL is considered as acceptable. This is why there are different MRL levels for different crops.

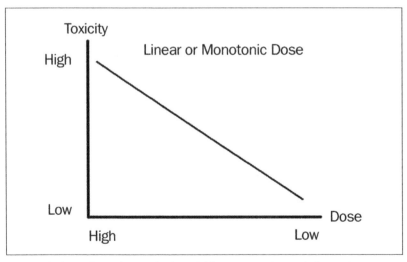

The graph above shows the standard model for toxicity of a steady linear decrease in the toxic effects in relation to the dose. The highest levels of toxic effects are at the highest doses. The toxic effect steadily decreases as the dose decreases.

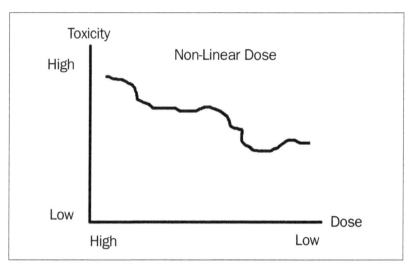

The graph above shows a non-linear dose. Instead of a predictable steady decrease of the toxicity in relation to the dose, as is found in the linear model, there can be an irregular decrease with areas where the toxicity stays around the same level, even though the dose is steadily decreasing.

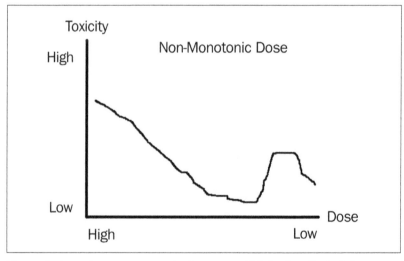

The graph above shows a non-monotonic response. This is where the toxicity may steadily decrease as the dose decreases; however, instead of continuing to decrease as the dose decreases like in the linear model, there is a point or points at which the toxicity can increase as the dose decreases.

The regulatory authorities then claim that any residue levels below the ADI or MRL are too low to cause health problems. This model is based on the assumption that the toxic effect decreases with the lower dosage in a steady linear progression until the compound is no longer toxic. It comes from the maxim of Paracelsus, the sixteenth-century physician and father of toxicology, who stated that, "All things are poison and nothing is without poison; only the dose makes a thing not a poison." This has been condensed to, "The dose makes the poison."

In the 1990s this five-hundred-year-old concept was proven incorrect for many chemicals through the endocrine disruption evidence presented in two books: *Our Stolen Future* and *The Feminization of Nature*. The peer-reviewed science summarized in these books showed that many chemicals, including agricultural chemicals, were mimicking hormones like estrogen.[2]

There are numerous exceptions to the assumption of a steady linear decrease in toxicity; one of the most profound is the evidence of non-monotonic responses in many chemicals when they start to act as hormones at very low levels.

The lowest doses of some chemicals can be more toxic instead of the least toxic. The current regulatory methodology of determining the ADI by lowering the threshold level of exposure is therefore problematic. This threshold is determined on the assumption that all chemicals including pesticides continue to decrease in toxicity in a linear model. Very little actual testing has been done at these levels to verify that this assumption is correct when setting the ADI.

A significant meta-review was published in 2012 by several of the world's leading expert scientists in this field in the peer-reviewed journal *Endocrine Reviews*. Vandenberg et al. showed that there were hundreds of published studies documenting non-monotonic and non-linear doses where chemicals were more toxic at low and often at the lowest doses.[3] The scientists stated:

> We provide a detailed discussion of the mechanisms responsible for generating these phenomena, plus hundreds of examples from the cell culture, animal, and epidemiology literature.

We illustrate that nonmonotonic responses and low-dose effects are remarkably common in studies of natural hormones and EDCs [endocrine-disrupting chemicals]. Whether low doses of EDCs influence certain human disorders is no longer conjecture, because epidemiological studies show that environmental exposures to EDCs are associated with human diseases and disabilities. We conclude that when nonmonotonic dose-response curves occur, the effects of low doses cannot be predicted by the effects observed at high doses.[4]

Evidence of non-monotonic dose response is of critical importance as it means that the ADIs and MRLs set for chemicals, including pesticides, have no actual scientific testing to determine that they do not adversely affect health outcomes by interfering with hormones. There are numerous studies showing that chemicals, including many pesticides, can be even more toxic at lower thresholds than the ADI, even though there were no observable adverse impacts at the higher dose levels that were used to set the NOAEL. Without testing, there is no way to know if the extrapolated assumptions used to set the ADI and consequently the MRL are correct and the recommendations safe.

No low safety threshold level should be assumed by extrapolating data from experiments done at higher doses. "Experimental data indicate that EDCs and hormones do not have NOAELs or threshold doses, and therefore no dose can ever be considered safe."[5] The WHO-UNEP meta-study on endocrine disruption clearly makes this point: "Endocrine disruptors produce nonlinear dose responses both in vitro [using components of an organism] and in vivo [living organisms in their normal state]; these non linear dose responses can be quite complex and often include non-monotonic dose responses. They can be due to a variety of mechanisms; because endogenous hormone levels fluctuate, no threshold can be assumed."[6] All the current ADIs and MRLs for pesticides need to undergo testing for endocrine disruption at the threshold levels that have been set by regulators to determine if they are truly safe.

THE ENDOCRINE SYSTEM

The endocrine system is based on numerous hormones that regulate the normal functioning and cycles of all living species, including humans. This includes reproductive hormones such as estrogen, progesterone, and testosterone; growth hormones such as somatrophin; metabolic hormones such as dopamine and thyroid-stimulating hormones; circadian-rhythm hormones like melatonin; and pancreatic hormones like insulin. There are numerous hormones or hormone-related compounds in all living species, and these need to be at the correct levels to ensure the good health and well-being of plants, animals, and humans. If the levels of any hormones are too high or too low, they can cause a wide variety of diseases. All living species have inbuilt regulatory systems to moderate hormone levels to ensure that they are in balance and in a state called homeostasis. Good health requires that homeostasis is maintained.

In the 1940s scientists began to notice that some pesticides produced hormonal changes in test animals. By the 1980s there were many studies showing that numerous chemicals, including pesticides, were causing significant hormonal changes in living species.

As an example, researchers have now found that there are many chemicals that act like reproductive hormones, such as estrogen, the main female hormone. There are other chemicals that can work against hormones, such as chemicals that interfere with testosterone, the male hormone. These are known as anti-androgens. These chemicals can cause a range of reproductive and other problems in potentially all species, including humans. There are numerous studies showing that very low doses of many common pesticides and numerous other chemicals disrupt the endocrine system by acting as or affecting hormones.

According to the WHO-UNEP study, these endocrine-disrupting chemicals are linked to a range of reproductive and other problems in humans. The

> **BY THE 1980s** *there were many studies showing that numerous chemicals, including pesticides, were causing significant hormonal changes in living species.*

ANNUAL INCIDENCE OF DIABETES (AGE ADJUSTED)

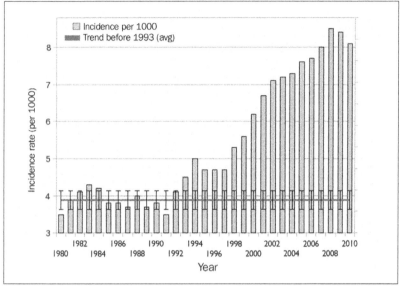

Sources: CDC, Courtesy of Dr. Nancy Swanson

AGE ADJUSTED DEATHS DUE TO OBESITY (ICD E66 & 278)

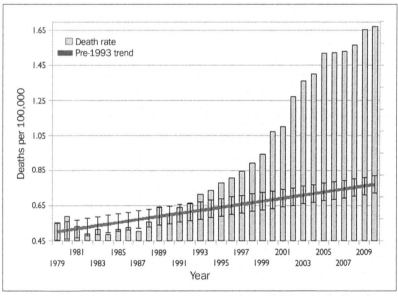

Sources: CDC, Courtesy of Dr. Nancy Swanson

AGE ADJUSTED THYROID CANCER INCIDENCE RATE

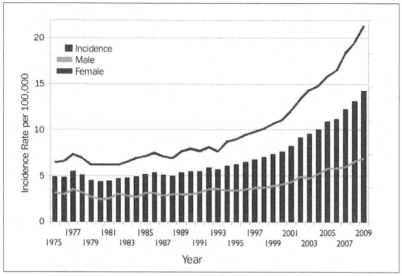

Source: NCI:SEER, Courtesy of Dr. Nancy Swanson

study found that up to 40 percent of young men in some countries have low semen quality. It also indicated an increase in genital malformations in baby boys such as undescended testes and penile malformations. These chemicals are also linked to an increase in adverse pregnancy outcomes such as preterm birth and low birth weight.

The increase in neurobehavioral disorders in children is associated with thyroid disruption. The age of breast development in girls is decreasing, and this is considered a risk factor for developing breast cancer later in life. Breast, endometrial, ovarian, prostate, testicular, and thyroid cancers are increasing. These are endocrine system-related cancers.

Obesity and type 2 diabetes levels have increased at a rapid rate around the world. There are 1.5 billion people who are overweight or obese, which is significantly more than the 850 million people who are undernourished. Between 1980 and 2008 the number of people with type 2 diabetes increased from 153 million to 347 million.[7] Increases in obesity and type 2 diabetes are linked to endocrine-disrupting chemicals interfering with normal hormonal metabolic processes in people.

A range of factors—such as diet, age, genetic makeup, sexually transmitted diseases, and exercise—contributes to the increases in reproductive problems; however, they only explain part of the increase. Numerous scientific studies show that EDCs cause these types of reproductive health problems in a wide range of animals, both in the wild and in laboratory research. Many scientists believe that ubiquitous exposure to EDCs is a significant reason for the increase in these widespread health problems. The WHO-UNEP meta-analysis stated:

> Moreover, effects of chemicals seen in exposed wildlife and in laboratory animals, similar to those seen in human populations and in DES-exposed individuals [diethylstilbestrol—a synthetic estrogen-mimicking chemical], have caused the scientific community to consider whether endocrine disruptors could also cause an increasing variety of reproductive health problems in women, including altered mammary gland development, irregular or longer fertility cycles, and accelerated puberty (Crain et al., 2008; Diamanti-Kandarakis et al., 2009; Woodruff et al., 2008). These changes indicate a higher risk of later health problems such as breast cancer, changes in lactation, or reduced fertility.[8]

Data from the International Agency for Research on Cancer (IARC), which is the specialized cancer agency of the WHO, showed an alarming rise in breast cancer rates in women. According to the IARC, "In 2012, 1.7 million women were diagnosed with breast cancer and there were 6.3 million women alive who had been diagnosed with breast cancer in the previous five years. Since the 2008 estimates, breast cancer incidence has increased by more than 20%, while mortality has increased by 14%. Breast cancer is also the most common cause of cancer death among women (522,000 deaths in 2012) and the most frequently diagnosed cancer among women in 140 of 184 countries worldwide."[9]

The latest overview of cancer in Australia, published in 2014 by the Australian Institute of Health and Welfare, showed that between 1982 and 2014, the number of new cancer cases diagnosed increased by 250 percent, from 47,417 to 123,920. This increase was mostly due to the rise in the incidence of breast cancer in females, prostate cancer in men, colorectal cancer, and lung cancer. Prostate and breast cancer are classic cancers of the endocrine system.

The researchers stated that the increase could be partly explained by the aging and increasing size of the population, improved diagnoses through population health screening programs, and improvements in technologies and techniques used to identify and diagnose cancer. However, as they stated, these reasons are only part of the explanation for the dramatic 250 percent increase over thirty years. The evidence quoted previously by the USPCP that 80 percent of cancers come from environmental causes, especially chemicals, is overwhelming. Endocrine-disrupting chemicals, including pesticides, have a documented role in this dramatic increase.[10]

Many researchers have found that although some of these synthetic chemicals were considered relatively safe in parts per million in the standard toxicology tests, at doses of parts per billion or parts

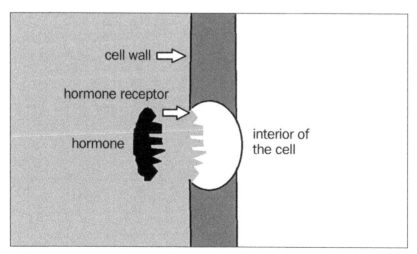

Each hormone receptor has a specific shape that allows the hormone to fit into it like a key in a lock. The specific shape of the receptor prevents other hormones or chemicals from fitting into it.

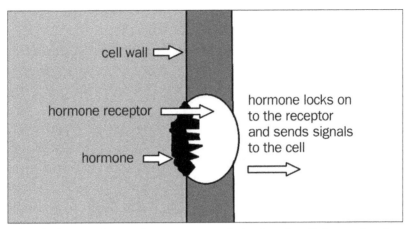

When the hormone fits into the receptor, it sends signals to the cell that regulates it. Hormones or chemicals of the wrong shape cannot fit into the receptor and therefore cannot send signals to the cell.

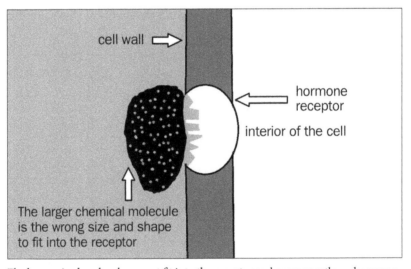

The larger-sized molecule cannot fit into the receptor and consequently no hormone signals are sent into the cell, so the cell is not disrupted with false instructions.

per trillion (more than a million times lower than parts per million) they acted like hormones. This was because at the very low levels they could attach to hormone receptors, whereas at higher levels they were "ignored" by the hormone receptors. When these chemicals attach to hormone receptors, they send signals to the endo-

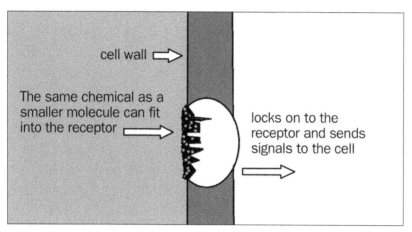

The same chemical as a smaller molecule can fit into the receptor and either send false signals to the cell or block the normal hormone signals, thereby disrupting the normal functioning of the cell.

crine system whereby they either act as the hormone, as an antagonist to the hormone, or block the normal working of the hormone. This disrupts the normal signaling functions of the hormone (endocrine) system and thus the name "endocrine disruptor." A good analogy for understanding how this process works is a lock on a door that can only be opened by a specifically shaped key. A metal rod larger than the key, if placed against the lock, cannot open the door because it is too large to fit into the lock. A smaller wire bent into the correct shape, although different in shape from the key, can work as a lock pick. The wire can also just sit in the lock and prevent the normal key from opening it.

Most receptors are shaped so that only the specific hormone can fit into them and act as the key to "unlock" them and send the signal that will activate the specific response in a cell, tissue, organ, or gene.

When chemicals are given in higher doses they, like the metal bar, cannot fit into the receptor, so they are ignored. Many chemicals at significantly lower doses are analogous to the thin wire lock pick. They can fit into the receptor and send out hormone signals or just block the normal hormone signals. Because they are not the actual hormone, these signals are artificial, and so they disrupt the normal hormone function.

THE EFFECT ON THE UNBORN AND GROWING CHILDREN

A large body of research shows that fetuses, newborns, and growing children are the most vulnerable group when exposed to low levels of EDCs. The WHO-UNEP meta-study found that there are "particularly vulnerable periods during fetal and postnatal life when EDCs alone, or in mixtures, have strong and often irreversible effects on developing organs, whereas exposure of adults causes lesser or no effects. Consequently, there is now a growing probability that maternal, fetal and childhood exposure to chemical pollutants play a larger role in the etiology of many endocrine diseases and disorders of the thyroid, immune, digestive, cardiovascular, reproductive and metabolic systems (including childhood obesity and diabetes) than previously thought possible."[11]

The fetus is most vulnerable during the times when genes are turned on to develop specific organs and systems. Small amounts of hormones signal genes to start developing various body parts and systems such as the reproductive tract, the nervous system, the brain, immune system, hormone systems, metabolic systems, limbs, etc. Small disruptions in these hormone signals can significantly alter the way these body parts and systems will develop, and these altered effects will not correct themselves.

> This does not diminish their [EDCs] importance [in adults], but contrasts with their effects in the fetus and neonate where a hormone can have permanent effects in triggering early developmental events such as cell proliferation or differentiation. Hormones acting during embryonic development can cause some structures to develop (e.g. male reproductive tract) or cause others to diminish (e.g. some sex-related brain regions). Once hormone action has taken place, at these critical times during development, the changes produced will last a lifetime.[12]

The actions of hormones on the development of endocrine and physiological systems in fetuses are considered to be programming events. They set how these systems will function in adults. "Thus, small perturbations in estrogen action during fetal development can change the reproductive axis in adulthood and diminish fertility (Mahoney and Padmanabhan, 2010). It is now clear that fetal programming events can predispose the adult to a number of chronic diseases (Janesick and Blumberg, 2011; Hanson and Gluckman, 2011); thus, endocrine disease prevention should begin with maternal and fetal health."[13]

This is why the unborn are far more vulnerable to endocrine-disrupting chemicals than adults and why testing must be undertaken to determine the effects on the fetus and not just on adult and adolescent animals as is currently done.

There are new testing methods using human cell cultures that can reduce, and in many cases end, the need for live animal testing, which is now being criticized due to humane and ethical issues. Because these cell lines come from humans, in many cases they can give more accurate results as well as sets of data that are not available from live animal testing.

> **A LARGE BODY OF RESEARCH** *shows that fetuses, newborns, and growing children are the most vulnerable group when exposed to low levels of EDCs.*

EXAMPLES OF A SMALL NUMBER OF THE HUNDREDS OF SCIENTIFIC STUDIES

The following are examples of a small number of the hundreds of scientific studies published on the effects of some of the common endocrine-disrupting pesticides and chemicals.

A study published in the peer-reviewed scientific journal *Food and Chemical Toxicology*, mentioned in chapter 1, found that glyphosate at residue levels commonly found in people induced human breast cancer cells to multiply. The scientists found that these low levels of glyphosate caused a five- to thirteenfold increase in the multiplication of estrogen-sensitive breast cancer cells; however they had no effect on non-estrogen-sensitive breast cancer cells. The majority of human breast cancers are sensitive to estrogen. This means that estrogen and compounds that act as estrogen cause these types of cancers to grow. The researchers state, "Glyphosate exerted proliferative effects only in human hormone-dependent breast cancer, T47D cells, but not in hormone independent breast cancer."[14]

One of the major concerns is that this activity occurred at residue levels of glyphosate that are commonly found in the urine of most people and below the current safety levels set by regulators. "Concentrations of glyphosate tested in this study that exhibited estrogenic activity and interfered with normal estrogen signaling were relevant to the range of concentrations that has been reported in environmental conditions and exposed humans. These results indicated that low and environmentally relevant concentrations of glyphosate possessed estrogenic activity."[15]

The scientists found that when these small levels of glyphosate in herbicides were combined with the normal levels of genistein, a phytoestrogen found in soybeans, it increased the multiplication of the breast cancer cells. The researchers concluded, "This study implied that the additive effect of glyphosate and genistein in post-menopausal women may induce cancer cell growth."[16]

THE SCIENTISTS FOUND *that when these small levels of glyphosate in herbicides were combined with the normal levels of genistein, a phytoestrogen found in soybeans, it increased the multiplication of the breast cancer cells.*

This additive effect is a great concern considering the vast increase in the planting of glyphosate-resistant GMO soybean varieties, which are now being widely used in soybean products such as soy milk, tofu, soy sauce, miso, etc. The scientists cited consuming these soybean products as a possible cause of breast cancer. "Furthermore, this study demonstrated the additive estrogenic effects of glyphosate and genistein which implied that the use of glyphosate-contaminated soybean products as dietary supplements may pose a risk of breast cancer because of their potential additive estrogenicity."[17]

Two peer-reviewed studies conducted by Hayes et al. showed that levels of atrazine, down to a level a thousand times lower than what's currently permitted in our food and in the environment, caused severe reproductive deformities in frogs.[18] Sara Storrs and Joseph Kiesecker of Pennsylvania State University confirmed Hayes's research. They exposed tadpoles of four frog species to atrazine and found that "Survival was significantly lower for all animals exposed to 3 ppb [parts per billion] compared with either 30 or 100 ppb. . . . These survival patterns highlight the importance of investigating the impacts of contaminants with realistic exposures and at various developmental stages."[19] These studies show that atrazine is a classic endocrine disrupter with a non-monotonic dose effect.

A study by Newbold et al. published in *Birth Defects Research* found that exposing pregnant mice to one part per billion of the synthetic estrogen mimic diethylstilbestrol (DES) can lead to offspring becoming severely obese in adulthood. Exposing the mice to 100 ppb DES resulted in the offspring being scrawny and underweight as adults.[20]

A scientific study published by Howdeshell et al. in the peer-reviewed journal *Nature* found that feeding pregnant mice 2.4 parts per billion of bisphenol A (BPA, an estrogenic plasticizing chemical used to make many plastic products including baby bottles and water bottles) on days eleven to seventeen of pregnancy resulted in the majority of the female offspring reaching sexual maturity earlier than the untreated females. The treated female offspring were also heavier than untreated females at sexual maturity. This is more than a thousand times lower than the fifty parts per million set by the U.S. EPA as safe.[21]

The study by Cavieres et al., published in 2002 in *Environmental Health Perspectives*, on the mixture of the common herbicides 2,4-D, mecoprop, dicamba, and inert ingredients showed that the greatest decrease in the number of embryos and live births in mice was at the lowest dosage level tested. The great concern is that the dose was one-seventh of the U.S. EPA level set for the drinking water.[22]

Skakkebaek et al. published a study in the journal *Human Reproduction* showing that a number of estrogenic and anti-androgenic chemicals, including common pesticides, are linked to abnormal changes in the development of the testes in the fetus. They found that these endocrine-disrupting chemicals were linked to the ever-increasing rate of genital urinary tract problems, deformities, and diseases such as undescended testes, low sperm counts, hypospadias, intersex, and testicular cancers.[23]

Studies show that pyrethroids are endocrine disruptors. Go et al. published a study in *Environmental Health Perspectives* that showed the estrogenic potential of certain pyrethroid compounds in the MCF-7 human breast carcinoma cell line promoted the increase in the proliferation of the cancer cells. Brander et al. published a study in *Environmental Toxicology and Chemistry* showing that pyrethroids can have both estrogenic and anti-estrogenic effects, which can lead to the disruption of the reproductive hormones in animals.[24]

THE IMPLICATIONS

The substantial body of published scientific research on endocrine disruption has several far-reaching implications. Firstly, the current methods of toxicology testing used to permit chemical residues in our food and water are based on the assumption that all chemicals lose their toxicity as their levels decrease to the point where they are nontoxic. This is clearly not correct for many chemicals. The USPCP report states, "Some scientists maintain that current toxicity testing and exposure limit-setting methods fail to accurately represent the nature of human exposure to potentially harmful chemicals. Current toxicity testing relies heavily on animal studies that utilize doses substantially higher than those likely to be encountered by humans."[25] This report clearly shows the need to test chemicals at the levels found in food, the environment, and most importantly in the human body.

Secondly, numerous published, peer-reviewed studies link the endocrine disruption caused by common commercially available chemicals to many of the health problems that are increasing in our society. These include the rise in obesity, type 2 diabetes, ADHD, depression, behavioral problems, cancers of the sexual tissues and endocrine system, and genital-urinary tract malformations, as well as lowered fertility rates and sperm counts.

Thirdly, the results of these studies show that the current regulatory systems cannot guarantee the safe use of chemicals. The vast majority of the synthetic chemicals used in our food supply and in our environment, including pesticides, have not been tested for endocrine disruption. The USPCP report stated that the current testing methodologies fail to detect harmful effects that may come from very low doses: "These data—and the exposure limits extrapolated from them—fail to take into account harmful effects that may occur only at very low doses."[26]

The WHO-UNEP meta-study raised the same issue about the current testing methodologies: "Close to 800 chemicals are known or suspected to be capable of interfering with hormone receptors, hormone synthesis or hormone conversion. However, only a small fraction of these chemicals have been investigated in tests capable of identifying overt endocrine effects in intact organisms."[27] The study expresses great concern over the fact that most of the thousands of synthetic chemicals have not been tested at all. The study authors expressed further concerns that the lack of testing means there is no credible scientific data that can validate that the current use of these chemicals is safe. "This lack of data introduces significant uncertainties about the true extent of risks from chemicals that potentially could disrupt the endocrine system."[28]

The meta-study by Vandenberg et al. stated that there is a need for changes in the methodologies used to test chemicals. Regulators need to take into account the possibility of non-monotonic dose responses when testing for safety rather than just assuming that the toxicity of all chemicals reduces as the dosage is lowered. Neglecting this possibility when testing commercially available chemicals poses serious hazards to human and environmental health. "Thus, fundamental changes in chemical testing and safety determination are needed to protect human health."[29] The WHO and UNEP meta-study also stated the need to change current methodologies so that tests can be developed for endocrine disruption.

The disturbing fact is that even though regulatory authorities have known of this information for more than thirty years, and even though many (including the U.S. EPA and the EFSA) are duty-bound to protect the public from risky chemicals, at the time of writing this book, only a select few, out of the eight hundred or so known endocrine disruptors, have been banned or restricted in use.

According to the Pesticide Action Network Europe, the European Commission is proposing to ban herbicides Amitrole and Isoproturon because of their endocrine disruption and other adverse toxic effects in September 2016. If this occurs, this will be the first time any pesticide has been banned for endocrine disruption anywhere in the world.

Amitrole is an endocrine disruptor that may damage unborn children, have toxic effects on reproductive organs and induce thyroid cancer while Isoproturon can cause adverse reproductive effects, gender bending and reduce fertility.[30]

Until thorough scientific testing is done on these chemicals and their effects on the endocrine system, regulatory authorities have no scientific basis or evidence supporting the assumption that exposure to chemical residues is safe at recommended levels. In light of the hundreds of studies showing non-monotonic dose curves in endocrine-disrupting chemicals, setting low thresholds for ADIs and MRLs by extrapolating data from testing animals at higher levels of exposure on the assumption that the toxicity will decrease in a steady linear model, is clearly not evidence-based science. It is decision making based on data-free assumptions, revealing that it is a myth that the residues are too low to cause any problems.

NOTES

[1] Bergman et al., *State of the Science of Endocrine Disrupting Chemicals 2012.*

[2] Colborn, Dumanoski, and Myers, *Our Stolen Future*; Cadbury, *Feminization of Nature.*

[3] Laura N. Vandenberg et al., "Hormones and Endocrine-Disrupting Chemicals: Low-Dose Effects and Nonmonotonic Dose Responses," *Endocrine Reviews* 33, no. 3 (June 2012): 378–455.

[4] Ibid.

[5] Ibid.

[6] Bergman et al., *State of the Science of Endocrine Disrupting Chemicals 2012.*

[7] Ibid.

[8] Ibid.

[9] "Latest World Cancer Statistics, Global Cancer Burden Rises to 14.1 Million New Cases in 2012: Marked Increase in Breast Cancers Must Be Addressed," International Agency for Research on Cancer and the World Health Organization, press release, December 12, 2013.

[10] Australian Institute of Health and Welfare, "Cancer in Australia: An Overview 2014," Cancer Series no. 90. Cat. no. CAN 88, Canberra: Australia, 2014.

[11] "Latest World Cancer Statistics," December 12, 2013.

[12] Ibid.

[13] Ibid.

[14] Siriporn Thongprakaisang et al., "Glyphosate Induces Human Breast Cancer Cells Growth via Estrogen Receptors," *Food and Chemical Toxicology* 59 (September 2013): 129–36, http://dx.doi.org/10.1016/j.fct.2013.05.057.

[15] Ibid.

[16] Ibid.

[17] Ibid.

[18] Tyrone B. Hayes et al., "Hermaphroditic, Demasculinized Frogs after Exposure to the Herbicide Atrazine at Low Ecologically Relevant Doses," *Proceedings of the National Academy of Sciences* 99, no. 8 (April 2002): 5476–80; Tyrone B. Hayes et al., "Atrazine-Induced Hermaphroditism at 0.1 ppb in American Leopard Frogs (*Rana pipiens*): Laboratory and Field Evidence," *Environmental Health Perspectives* 111, no. 4 (April 2003): 569–75.

[19] Sara I. Storrs and Joseph M. Kiesecker, "Survivorship Patterns of Larval Amphibians Exposed to Low Concentrations of Atrazine," *Environmental Health Perspectives* 112, no. 10 (July 2004): 1054–57.

[20] Retha R. Newbold et al., "Developmental Exposure to Estrogenic Compounds and Obesity," *Birth Defects Research Part A: Clinical and Molecular Teratology* 73, no. 7 (2005): 478–480.

[21] Kembra Howdeshell et al., "Environmental Toxins: Exposure to Bisphenol A Advances Puberty," *Nature* 401 (October 1999): 762–64.

[22] Cavieres, "Developmental Toxicity of a Commercial Herbicide Mixture in Mice."

[23] N. E. Skakkebæk, E. Rajpert-De Meyts, and K. M. Main, "Testicular Dysgenesis Syndrome: An Increasingly Common Developmental Disorder with Environmental Aspects," *Human Reproduction* 16, no. 5 (2001): 972–78.

[24] Go et al., "Estrogenic Potential of Certain Pyrethroid Compounds; Brander et al., "The In Vivo Estrogenic and In Vitro Anti-Estrogenic Activity of Permethrin and Bifenthrin."

[25] "U.S. President's Cancer Panel Annual Report," 2010.

[26] Ibid.

[27] Bergman et al., eds., *State of the Science of Endocrine Disrupting Chemicals 2012.*

[28] Ibid.

[29] Vandenberg et al., "Hormones and Endocrine-Disrupting Chemicals."

[30] "EU Commission Proposes Its First Bans for Endocrine Disrupting Pesticides." Pesticide Action Network. April 14, 2016. http://www.pan-europe.info/sites/pan-europe.info/files/public/resources/press-releases/pan-press-release-scopaff-apr-16.pdf.

MYTH 3

"Breakdown"

"Modern pesticides rapidly biodegrade."

One of the major pesticide legends is the belief that most modern agricultural chemicals rapidly biodegrade and leave few, if any, residues. We are misled into believing that they break down and do not persist in our food like older chemicals such as DDT.

The following is a claim by the main food regulator in Australia and New Zealand, FSANZ, and is typical of the claims by many nations' regulators. They state, "Organophosphorus pesticides, carbamate pesticides are mostly biodegradable, and therefore do not concentrate in the food chain. Synthetic pyrethroids . . . are generally biodegradable and therefore tend not to persist in the environment."[1] These types of statements give the false impression that few agricultural pesticides persist in our food and environment. In fact, most agricultural and veterinary chemicals leave residues in food. That is the reason tolerances for maximum residue limits (MRLs) and the acceptable daily intake (ADI) are set for these poisons.

The data presented in the United States President's Cancer Panel (USPCP) 2010 report indicating that only 23.1 percent of food samples had zero pesticide residues, is reasonably consistent with the data from testing in most countries. This means that the overwhelming majority of foods contain pesticide residues.

Many of the current chemicals, including some of the synthetic pyrethroids, organophosphates, carbamates, and herbicides such as atrazine, are as residual as the mostly banned older chemicals such as the organochlorine group that includes dieldrin, DDT, chlordane, heptachlor, lindane, and aldrin.

METABOLITES OF PESTICIDES

One of the biggest myths is the assumption that once a chemical degrades it disappears and is harmless. Most agricultural poisons leave residues of breakdown products or daughter chemicals when they degrade.[2] These breakdown products of chemicals are also called metabolites. Where there is research, it shows that many of the metabolites from agricultural poisons cause health and reproductive problems.

A substantial number of agricultural pesticides—such as organophosphates like diazinon, malathion, chlorpyrifos, and dimethoate—become even more toxic when they break down. The metabolites of organophosphates are known as oxons. Scientists at the Cooperative Wildlife Research Laboratory at Southern Illinois University and the Western Ecology Research Center of the U.S. Geological Survey in Point Reyes, California, found that oxons can be up to a hundred times more toxic than the original pesticide.

> In this study the oxon derivatives of chlorpyrifos, malathion, and diazinon were significantly more toxic than their respective parental forms. Chloroxon killed all of *R. boylii* tadpoles and was at least 100 times more [toxic] than the lowest concentration of chlorpyrifos which resulted in no mortality. Maloxon was nearly 100 times more toxic than malathion and diazoxon was approximately 10 times more toxic than its parent. This is consistent with other studies that have compared parent and oxon forms.[3]

Oxons

Studies have shown that many pesticides used in agriculture, such as diazinon, malathion, chlorpyrifos, and dimethoate, become even more dangerous to the environment as they break down into metabolites called oxons. Oxons result when a chemical bond between phosphorus and sulfur is replaced by a bond between phosphorus and oxygen as the pesticide breaks down in the environment. Oxons can cause significant damage to animals' nervous systems.

Dimethoate is a good example. Dimethoate is a systemic pesticide because it is absorbed into all the tissues of the plant, including the edible portions such as all the flesh of fruits, stems, tubers, and leaves.

Contrary to popular belief, because systemic poisons are absorbed into the flesh—and consequently every part of the plant is toxic—washing or peeling the surface of the food only removes a small percentage of the poisons on the surface. It will not remove the bulk of poison, which is inside the food.

Dimethoate is widely used as a fruit fly treatment because it is so residual that even after two weeks any maggots that hatch from eggs inside the fruit will be killed by the poison residues in the edible portion of the flesh. Dimethoate breaks down to an even more toxic metabolite called omethoate. Omethoate is also used as a pesticide and consequently, unlike the vast majority of metabolites, it has been researched and has an LD_{50}. According to the WHO, omethoate has an LD_{50} of 50 milligrams per kilogram, whereas dimethoate has an LD_{50} of 150 milligrams per kilogram. This means that as the dimethoate decays within the treated food, it becomes 300 percent more toxic as omethoate. Under the WHO classification of hazards it goes from being a moderately hazardous to a highly hazardous pesticide. Several countries have withdrawn or are in the process of withdrawing omethoate from use as a pesticide due to its high toxicity and its persistence. Other countries are still debating whether to ban dimethoate. All food that is treated with dimethoate will end up with residues of the more toxic and persistent omethoate as well as a number of other toxic metabolites that are generated as the dimethoate breaks down.

In her article "A Case for Revisiting the Safety of Pesticides," Dr. Theo Colborn gives the example of research into paraoxon, the main metabolite of parathion, showing that it is very toxic and causes a range of negative health effects. "Chronic paraoxon exposure (0.1, 0.15, or 0.2 mg/kg subcutaneously) during a stage of rapid cholinergic brain development from PND8 to PND20 [various stages of prenatal development] in male Wistar rats led to reduced dendritic spine density in the hippocampus without obvious toxic cholinergic signs in any of the animals (Santos et al. 2004). Some animals in the two highest dose groups died in the early days of the study. All doses caused retarded perinatal growth, and brain cholinesterase activity was reduced 60% by PND21."[4]

ALL FOOD THAT IS TREATED *with dimethoate will end up with residues of the more toxic and persistent omethoate as well as a number of other toxic metabolites that are generated as the dimethoate breaks down.*

Glyphosate is another example. It breaks down into the more persistent aminomethylphosphonic acid (AMPA) that has been linked to liver disease.[5]

A scientific study published in the journal *Annals of Allergy, Asthma & Immunology* found that exposure to dichlorophenols was linked to an increase in food allergies. Dichlorophenols are metabolites of chlorinated pesticides such as 2,4-D, dichlorvos, and chlorpyrifos, and they are found in chlorinated drinking water. The researchers concluded that, "High urine levels of dichlorophenols are associated with the presence of sensitization to foods in a U.S. population. Excessive use of dichlorophenols may contribute to the increasing incidence of food allergies in westernized societies."[6]

Additional examples include the desnitro or descyano metabolites of neonicotinoids. They are significantly more toxic to mammals than the parent pesticide.[7]

IMPURITIES IN PESTICIDES

Pesticide testing is done with pure, laboratory-grade active ingredients and not with actual ingredients from the mass-manufacturing process. Manufacturing processes can result in the creation of a number of by-products, many of which can be toxic. According to the USPCP, "Other industrial chemicals or processes have hazardous by-products or metabolites. Numerous chemicals used in manufacturing remain in or on the product as residues, while others are integral components of the products themselves."[8] These by-products are largely ignored by regulatory authorities based on the assumption that, because they are at such low levels, they are safe. However where there has been testing, some of these impurities have been found to be highly toxic.

Dioxins, or more correctly polychlorinated dibenzodioxins (PCDDs), are examples of some of the most common impurities. PCDDs are commonly called dioxins because their primary molecules have dioxin skeletal rings. There are potentially hundreds of dioxins, most of which have had limited testing. Dioxins are one of the major groups of metabolites that result from chemical processes that use chlorine. These can include chlorine bleaching fibers for paper or textiles, the wood preservative pentachlorophenol, herbicides such as 2,4-D, insecticides such chlorpyrifos, and chlorinated fertilizers such as muriate of potash.

Dioxins can be generated by burning or heating substances that contain chlorine, as in municipal and hospital wastes and crop residues that have been treated with pesticides containing chlorine. Some of the major emitters are sugar mills that burn the crop residues that have been treated with chlorinated pesticides and fertilizers.

Dioxins are some of the most toxic chemicals known to science and can cause a wide variety of illnesses, especially cancers and birth defects. Chlorine is a common ingredient in many pesticides due to its toxicity and its residual persistence. Consequently, many pesticides will contain dioxins and/or dioxins will be created as metabolites when they degrade.

Dioxins are also endocrine disrupters, and according to the study by the WHO and UNEP they cause sex ratio imbalances in humans and wildlife, resulting in fewer males. "EDC-related sex ratio imbalances, resulting in fewer male offspring in humans, do exist (e.g., in relation to dioxin and 1,2-dibromo-3-chloropropane), although the underlying mechanisms are unknown. The effects of dioxin on sex ratio are now corroborated by results obtained in the mouse model."[9]

Agent Orange, an herbicide that was widely used to destroy the highly biodiverse rainforests in Vietnam and Laos during the Vietnam War, was the best known of the chemicals contaminated with dioxins. Agent Orange was a combination of two herbicides: 2,4-D and 2,4,5-T. The manufacturing process of 2,4,5-T resulted in very high levels of dioxins, particularly 2,3,7,8-tetrachlorodibenzo-p-dioxin (TCDD). This was the reason it was banned. However 2,4-D continues to be widely used despite being contaminated with TCDD, one of the most toxic and carcinogenic molecules known to humans.

As Vallianatos states, "TCDD initiates and promotes cancer at a potency 17 million times greater than that of benzene, 5 million times greater than carbon tetrachloride, and a hundred thousand times greater than PCBs. TCDD bioaccumulates in animals at dramatic rates: twenty thousand times greater than benzene, six thousand times greater than carbon tetrachloride, and four times greater than PCBs."[10]

The herbicide 2,4-D also contains other dioxins. These dioxins are present as impurities from the manufacturing processes; however, they can also be formed as metabolites as the 2,4-D decays.

Dioxins are very persistent in the environment, and consequently Vietnam still has extremely high levels of the environmental contamination resulting in birth defects, immune diseases, cancers, and many other problems more than forty years after the widespread use of Agent Orange was stopped.

Dioxins are pervasive throughout the global environment and are found in the tissues of most living species, especially in species at the top of the food chain, such as humans, as they bioaccumulate. In some cases they can come from natural causes, such as active volcanoes and forest fires; however, the bulk of dioxins are by-products of the chemical industry. Some of the most infamous cases are Love Canal, New York; Times Beach, Missouri; and the massive release from an industrial accident in Seveso, Italy. The attempted assassination of President Viktor Yushchenko of Ukraine by poisoning with dioxins in 2004 resulted in permanent health problems. Due to a lack of research, however, the full extent of the contribution of the numerous chlorinated pesticides to the widespread global contamination by dioxins in the environment and the tissues of most living species has not been determined.

Research by Mesnage et al. published in 2015 found residues of TCDD in commercial animals' feeds. These feeds come from the same crops used to feed humans, so it is reasonable to assume that people eating food from farming systems that use 2,4-D and other chlorinated pesticides and fertilizers are being exposed to levels of TCDD that can cause cancer. The herbicide 2,4-D should have been banned when 2,4,5-T was banned. The latter was banned because it contains TCCD—so why is 2,4-D still allowed?

The greatest concern, according to the U.S. National Institute of Environmental Health Sciences (NIEHS), is that most people are exposed to dioxins from food, "in particular animal products, contaminated by these chemicals. Dioxins are absorbed and stored in fat tissue and, therefore, accumulate in the food chain. More than 90 percent of human exposure is through food."[11] Examples include dioxins being found in mozzarella cheese in Italy and in pork in Ireland in 2008 and in animal feed in Germany in 2010. Instead of taking the contamination from impurities into account when assessing the negative health effects of pesticides, regulators do the opposite. They reject the studies based on the belief that these extra chemicals confound the data.

In chapter 1, I mentioned IARC's review that classified the herbicide 2,4-D as a possible carcinogen. The IARC review states, "Due to the potential for confounding, studies involving exposure to mixed herbicides or to herbicides containing dioxin were regarded as uninformative about the carcinogenicity of 2,4-D."[12] Consequently, IARC dismissed these studies and did not consider them even though they showed a link between 2,4-D and cancer in humans.

Regulators need to test and review the actual products used as these are the ones that affect people's health, not the laboratory-grade pure chemicals that are not used in agriculture.

LACK OF COMPLETE TESTING IN FOOD RESIDUE SURVEYS

To the knowledge of this author, no country in the world has tested food for every pesticide used. Most only test for a "representative sample" of commonly used pesticides and ignore the vast majority of hundreds of permitted pesticides. For example, most national residue monitoring programs do not test for glyphosate due to the difficulty posed by testing for it, despite the fact that it is the most commonly used pesticide in the world. The USDA has never tested food for glyphosate residues. Only a few European countries have tested for it and have found it in a variety of foods. In the UK, glyphosate and its main metabolite AMPA have been found in over 30 percent of bread and 50 percent of grain samples.[13]

There is very little testing done to detect the residues of the metabolites and by-products of agricultural poisons in our food and water. There is virtually no testing for the "inerts" even though most of them are toxic. At best, only a few select metabolites are tested for and the majority are ignored. The 23 percent of food in the United States that was found with no residues could still be toxic for two reasons.

Firstly, the 23 percent of food with no residue is largely meaningless if the testing does not include 100 percent of pesticides used in food production. How can the regulators claim that the food is free of residues or that the residue levels are safe if they have not tested for every possible residue? How can these safety tests be considered credible when they leave out glyphosate, the most commonly used herbicide? Secondly, just because the testing didn't find the parent chemical does not mean that it is free of the toxic residues of the metabolites or the toxic by-products like dioxins that can result from the manufacturing of pesticides and toxic "inerts" such as cancer-causing petroleum distillates. All it means is that there has been no testing for them.

MORE RESEARCH NEEDED TO DETERMINE METABOLITE SAFETY

Very little research has been done to determine safe intake levels for the metabolites or the by-products of agricultural poisons. Consequently, there are very few safety levels to determine the ADI for the numerous toxic metabolites and by-products that contaminate our food. Very little research has been done about the effects of metabolites and impurities on the developing fetus, newborns, and growing children. These age groups are particularly sensitive to toxins, and in the case of endocrine disruptors and nerve poisons, the science shows that there are no safe levels. The research that has been done on metabolites of nerve poisons from organophosphates, neonicotinoids, pyrethroids and dioxins and endocrine disrupters shows very serious implications for the normal development of children.

VERY LITTLE RESEARCH *has been done to determine safe intake levels for the metabolites or the by-products of agricultural poisons.*

The toxicity and health effects of pesticide metabolites and impurities are mostly ignored on an assumption that they are safe. The regulation of pesticides is supposed to be based on science and evidence. Until research is conducted into the toxicity and persistence of all metabolites and impurities of pesticides and published in peer-reviewed journals, regulatory authorities have no peer-reviewed, science-based evidence to show that any of the current residue levels in food or in the environment are safe. Ignoring them or assuming that they are safe cannot be regarded as an acceptable regulatory practice. Regulatory authorities have a duty of care to ensure that the general population and especially children are not harmed by these toxic chemicals and not perpetuate myths about their safety.

NOTES

[1] Food Standards Australia and New Zealand, "20th Australian Total Diet Survey."

[2] Short, *Quick Poison, Slow Poison*; Colborn, Dumanoski, and Myers, *Our Stolen Future*; Cadbury, *Feminization of Nature*; Cox, "Glyphosate (Roundup)"; Colborn, "A Case for Revisiting the Safety of Pesticides."

[3] D. W. Sparling, Gary Fellers. "Comparative Toxicity of Chlorpyrifos, Diazinon, Malathion and Their Oxon Derivatives to Larval *Rana boylii*," *Environmental Pollution* 147 (2007): 535–39.

[4] Colborn, "A Case for Revisiting the Safety of Pesticides."

[5] Cox, "Glyphosate (Roundup)."

[6] Elina Jerschow et al., "Dichlorophenol-Containing Pesticides and Allergies: Results from the U.S. National Health and Nutrition Examination Survey 2005–2006," *Annals of Allergy, Asthma & Immunology* 109, no. 6 (December 2012): 420–25.

[7] Motohiro Tomizawa, "Neonicotinoids and Derivatives: Effects in Mammalian Cells and Mice," Jou*rnal of Pesticide Science* 29, no. 3 (2004): 177–83.

[8] "U.S. President's Cancer Panel Annual Report," 2010.

[9] Bergman et al., *State of the Science of Endocrine Disrupting Chemicals 2012*.

[10] Vallianatos, *Poison Spring*.

[11] National Institute of Environmental Health Sciences, http://www.niehs.nih.gov (accessed July 15, 2013).

[12] "Glyphosate," IARC Monographs–112.

[13] Ibid.

The myth that should be of immense concern to all of us is that government regulatory authorities ensure that agricultural poisons are used safely. According to an EPA statement in the USDA news release for its 2013 Pesticide Data Program, as parents we should have no concerns because the main pesticide regulator in the United States claims to have "a rigorous, science-based, and transparent regulatory program for pesticides that continues to protect people's health and the environment."[1]

Some countries have or are about to have food safety regulations that require farmers to be trained in using chemicals and keeping records of their use. There are private or market-based food safety schemes with similar, and in some cases, stricter requirements.

However, most of the approximately 206 nations in the world (including observer and disputed states) do not have adequate regulatory systems that monitor whether agricultural poisons are used as directed by the label and as per "good agricultural practices." This is a major issue in the developing world where most farmers have a limited or no ability to read or write. In many cases they have to rely on the advice from local sales agents as to which pesticide to use, the rate it is mixed with water, and the amount to use on the crop. Quite often the local sales agent has limited literacy and numeracy as well and does not have the technical knowledge to give this advice. In other cases they corruptly sell whatever pesticide they have in stock and give erroneous advice.

Most farmers in the developing world rarely use safety equipment like face masks or protective clothing and gloves. In some cases they mix the pesticide with water, stir it with their bare hands, and then splash it over the plants from a bucket without wearing gloves because they cannot afford spray equipment or protective clothing. In other cases this is done because the farmers do not understand that the chemicals are toxic to humans. For instance, in many parts of India the word for pesticide is *dawai*, which means medicine in Hindi. Toxic synthetic pesticides are marketed and sold as "medicine for plants," so many of India's 600 million farmers actually think that they are healthy rather than highly dangerous. Rural farmers across the globe store and mix the chemicals in their small huts, surrounded by family members and next to their food. Consequently, the highest rates of pesticide poisonings are among farmers, their families, farm workers, and in rural communities in the developing world.

> **TOXIC SYNTHETIC PESTICIDES** *are marketed and sold as "medicine for plants," so many of India's 600 million farmers actually think that they are healthy rather than highly dangerous.*

In *Poisoning Our Future*, Dr. Watts devotes several chapters to the extensive harm caused by the everyday use of pesticides to people in farming communities around the world, particularly in developing countries. She cites volumes of published science showing how exposure to pesticides is severely harming the children of farming families.

Dr. Vandana Shiva and her colleagues Dr. Mira Shiva and Dr. Vaibhav Singh in their book, *Poisons in Our Food*, give numerous examples of how the misuse of pesticides in India is causing an epidemic of serious diseases. The book summarizes research linking disease epidemics like cancer and severe birth defects to the use of pesticides in Indian agriculture. They discuss how the widespread use of endosulfan in Kerala contributes to numerous birth defects in children, and how Punjab, the state of the Green Revolution's birth in India, is currently in the midst of a cancer epidemic that is killing tens of thousands of people. The amount of people suffering from this disease has increased so much that there is a dedicated and infamous Cancer Train needed to transport thousands of people to hospitals for cancer treatment.[2]

FARM PESTICIDE USE MONITORING IS GROSSLY INADEQUATE

Even developed countries and regions that have government regulatory systems, such as the United States, Australia, and the European Union, have serious issues in how regulations are administered. Vallianatos, in his book *Poison Spring*, points out many of these deficiencies, especially the fact that most regulators have very little knowledge about how modern industrial farming works and make data-free assumptions about how farmers apply pesticides.

> A 1981 government survey of agricultural practices in Florida showed, for example, that in about 40% of cases, farmers used the wrong spray on a given crop, or simply used too much. Such basic, misinformed behavior destroys any chance of producing safe food and essentially renders EPA's regulations meaningless.

> The situation has been made worse by weakening—or outright elimination—of the EPA's monitoring capabilities.[3]

Most developed countries and some developing countries have monitoring programs to test the food sold in shops and markets for residues that exceed the maximum residue limits (MRLs). In most cases the residues are below the MRLs. The conclusion is that because most of the pesticide residues are below the MRLs the usage is safe, and consumers are safe because the food residues are within the acceptable safety margins.

However, as shown by the information in the previous chapters, these MRLs are highly questionable as they have been based on outdated methodologies that do not test for:
- Mixtures and cocktails of chemicals
- The actual formulated product
- The metabolites, inerts, and impurities of pesticides
- The special requirements of the fetus and the newborn
- Endocrine disruption
- Intergenerational effects
- Developmental neurotoxicity
- Epigenetic changes

History shows that regulatory authorities have consistently failed to prevent the contamination of the environment and human health by-products previously designated safe, such as arsenic, asbestos, lead, mercury, dioxins, PCBs, DDT, dieldrin, and other persistent organic pollutants. In many cases these products are still widely used, such as mercury in tooth fillings, preservatives in vaccines, and fungicides in agriculture. DDT is still employed in countries like Uganda and China. Lead paint and white asbestos are still widely used in many countries. For the few products that have been withdrawn, it happened only decades after good scientific evidence demonstrated that they are harmful.

The American Academy of Pediatrics in their 2011 Policy Statement, *Chemical-Management Policy: Prioritizing Children's Health*, criticized how the EPA was administering The Toxic Substance Control Act (TSCA) passed in 1976. "It is widely recognized to have been ineffective in protecting children, pregnant women, and the general population from hazardous chemicals in the marketplace. It does not take into account the special vulnerabilities of children in attempting to protect the population from chemical hazards. Its processes are so cumbersome that in its more than 30 years of existence, the TSCA has been used to regulate only 5 chemicals or chemical classes of the tens of thousands of chemicals that are in commerce."

The authors of the policy statement were highly critical of the way the EPA managed many key programs: "For example, the Endocrine Disruptor Screening Program was called for in legislation passed in 1996, but the EPA only issued its first test orders, the first step in a multistep process, in October 2009. The Voluntary Children's Chemical Evaluation Program was launched by the EPA at the end of 2000. It had the meager goal of gathering information on health effects, exposure, risk, and data needs for 23 chemicals to which children have a high likelihood of exposure. More than a decade later, for various reasons, complete data are not available for any of those chemicals."[4]

Regulatory authorities around the world are disregarding a large body of published science conducted by hundreds of trained scientists and experts in these fields that clearly shows that the current methods of determining the safety of the agricultural poisons are grossly inadequate.

REGULATORY PROCESSES

Vallianatos worked in the EPA, the main regulatory authority of the United States, for twenty-five years. His book about his time in the EPA, *Poison Spring*, is an exposé on the corruption of the regulatory process, shedding light on how the pesticide industry has unduly influenced decision-making processes.

"The agency has become a toothless tiger, only pretending to fight on behalf of the environment and public health. EPA officials know global chemical and agribusiness industries are manufacturing science. They know their products are dangerous. Yet industry power either corrupts or silences EPA scientists, who are forced then to bury or ignore the truth. Scientists find themselves working in a roomful of funhouse mirrors, plagiarizing industry studies and cutting and pasting the findings of industry as their own."[5]

Of great concern is the massive conflict of interest of the "revolving door," in which former managers and attorneys of pesticide corporations get senior jobs in the EPA. Once employed in the EPA, they have the power to make regulatory decisions to approve the products of their former employers. Similarly, EPA managers are given senior positions in pesticide corporations and influence their former colleagues in the EPA. This corrupt and unethical behavior is like putting the fox in charge of the henhouse and is a massive conflict of interest.

THE WHO AND UNEP *meta-study clearly states that the current regulatory systems are inadequate when it comes to the issue of endocrine-disrupting chemicals.*

Dr. Theo Colborn gives examples that show that the EPA is ignoring a wealth of peer-reviewed scientific studies and is largely basing its conclusions on unpublished studies that have been commissioned by the pesticide industry. "Although this information is available, the U.S. EPA has rarely used the open literature in its risk assessments, generally using only data submitted by manufacturers."[6]

She states that by only relying on the data provided by pesticide manufacturers, the EPA is missing nearly all the delayed developmental, morphologic, and functional damage to the fetus. They are also missing data on the way pesticides interfere with the physiological systems in humans. "For example, Brucker-Davis (1998) published a comprehensive review of the open literature in which she found 63 pesticides that interfere with the thyroid system—a system known for more than a century to control brain development, intelligence, and behavior. Yet, to date, the U.S. EPA has never taken action on a pesticide because of its interference with the thyroid system."[7]

The WHO and UNEP meta-study clearly states that the current regulatory systems are inadequate when it comes to the issue of endocrine-disrupting chemicals. "We cannot be confident that the current system of protecting human and wildlife population from chemicals with endocrine activity is working as well as it should to help prevent adverse health impacts on human and wildlife populations."[8]

The USPCP report was critical about the current testing methodologies and the lack of action taken by regulatory authorities in reviewing the toxicity of chemicals based on the latest peer-reviewed science:

> The prevailing regulatory approach in the United States is reactionary rather than precautionary. That is, instead of taking preventive action when uncertainty exists about the potential harm a chemical or other environmental contaminant may cause, a hazard must be incontrovertibly demonstrated before action to ameliorate it is initiated. Moreover, instead of requiring industry or other proponents of specific chemicals, devices, or activities to prove their safety, the public bears the burden of proving that a given environmental exposure is harmful.[9]

Dr. Nancy Swanson and Dr. Mae-Wan Ho reviewed the decision-making process of the European Union (EU) regulator conducting the Risk Assessment Report (RAR) on the safety of glyphosate. The German Federal Institute for Risk Assessment (BfR, or Bundesinstitut für Risikobewertung) is responsible for the RAR. According to Swanson and Ho, "There is no information on authorship anywhere within the 15 documents totaling 3,744 pages. Between April and June of 2014, the BfR was contacted and asked on four separate occasions to provide information on who authored the report and which committee at BfR was responsible for the report. To date, they have not responded."[10]

Swanson and Ho also documented how employees of pesticide companies influence regulatory decisions about their company products by having seats on the regulatory decision-making committees, a gross conflict of interest. "The BfR Committee for Pesticides and Their Residues (CPTR), which might be expected to be responsible for preparing the RAR, has 3 out of 12 of its 2014 members and 4 out of its 16 2011–2013 members from either BASF or Bayer CropScience. This serious conflict of interest in a regulatory agency is not restricted to BfR, it is endemic to the EU regulatory agency."

Like Vallianatos documented in his book on the EPA, a "revolving door" also exists in the European Union regulatory process, in which people with ties to the pesticide industry make the regulatory decisions about the industry products. Swanson and Ho reported that the majority of people on the scientific panel of the main European regulator, the European Food Safety Authority (EFSA), had links to industry. "The Corporate Europe Observatory report 'Unhappy Meal' published in October 2013, revealed that some 59% of EFSA's scientific panel members still had direct or indirect links to companies whose activities fell under EFSA's remit. As a result, the European Parliament voted in April 2014 for a resolution to ban scientists with ties to the agriculture and food industries from working at the agency, and has given EFSA two years to clean up its act."[11]

While it is good news that the European Parliament has given EFSA two years to end this gross conflict of interest, according to Swanson and Ho it has not stopped the culture where, like the EPA, EFSA is still engaging in obvious conflicts of interest relying too heavily on industry sponsored studies and experts. They found that the bulk of the European Risk Assessment Report was based on the document submitted by the Glyphosate Task Force (GTF), a pesticide industry organization that is composed of various European chemical companies and Monsanto. Swanson and Ho stated, "But the conflict of interest is even more blatant than anyone could have imagined. It is Monsanto and a consortium of European chemical companies that performed the risk assessment for the re-approval of glyphosate."

Steven Druker, in his well-researched book *Altered Genes, Twisted Truth: How the Venture to Genetically Engineer Our Food Has Subverted Science, Corrupted Government, and Systematically Deceived the Public*, gives numerous examples how the same companies manipulated the science around GMOs and the regulatory processes so these novel crops were approved with little or no testing.[12]

Druker's and Vallianatos's books are well worth reading to understand how science, scientists, regulators, policy makers, and the mainstream media are corrupted or manipulated into disregarding evidence-based, peer-reviewed, published science and warnings from experts and instead supporting decisions that are clearly endangering the health of the environment, the general population, and especially our children.

THE EPA, EFSA, AND GLYPHOSATE

Both the EPA and EFSA recently reviewed glyphosate and approved large increases in its ADIs and MRLs in our food and environment. When doing so, both regulators stated that there was no evidence that glyphosate caused cancer. However in March 2015, the WHO's IARC classified glyphosate as a carcinogen based on several scientific studies linking it to a range of cancers including non-Hodgkin's lymphoma, renal cancers, skin cancers, and pancreatic cancer. The IARC initially published its conclusion in the *Lancet Oncology Journal*, the world's premier scientific journal for cancer studies.

Seventeen independent experts from eleven countries reviewed the scientific studies and gave glyphosate the second highest classification of 2A. IARC has five classifications for the carcinogenicity of substances:

- Group 1: Carcinogenic to humans
- Group 2A: Probably carcinogenic to humans
- Group 2B: Possibly carcinogenic to humans
- Group 3: Unclassifiable as to carcinogenicity in humans
- Group 4: Probably not carcinogenic to humans

Group 1 is for substances like tobacco, alcohol, asbestos, and benzene, where numerous scientific studies have shown that they cause cancer in humans. Only around a hundred substances out over nine hundred studied have been placed in this category.

Group 2A is for substances that have sufficient evidence of causing cancer in animals and limited studies in humans. According to IARC, the 2A classification was given because, "strong mechanistic evidence; for malathion and glyphosate, the mechanistic evidence provided independent support of the 2A classification based on evidence of carcinogenicity in humans and experimental animals."[13]

In 1985, the U.S. EPA classified glyphosate as a carcinogen. In 1991 the U.S. EPA reviewed the studies and, in the opinion of Swanson and Ho and other experts, manipulated the interpretation of the data to claim that there was no evidence of cancer. Three members of the EPA review committee refused to endorse the final document, with two members writing that they did not concur with the conclusion. The latest review by the experts of IARC committee concluded that several of these early studies did in fact show clear evidence that glyphosate causes cancer.[14]

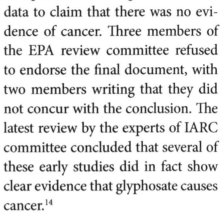

IT IS A HUGE CONFLICT OF INTEREST *that representatives of organizations with direct or indirect economic interests from the sales or use of pesticides should be allowed to make the decisions on whether these products should be restricted or banned.*

The IARC classification of glyphosate as a carcinogen contradicted the conclusion of the German BfR. The BfR stated that glyphosate did not cause cancer and that it was so safe that they recommended that EFSA approve huge increases in the ADIs and MRLs. In order to resolve this contradiction, EFSA asked BfR to review their decision. The BfR did this and once again concluded that glyphosate was unlikely to cause cancer in humans.[15]

This decision should not come as a surprise, given Swanson and Ho documented how employees of pesticide companies sat on the BfR Committee for Pesticides and Their Residues (CPTR). The French investigative journalist Stéphane Foucart, writing in Le Monde, confirmed that several members of the BfR CPTR are employed by the chemical industry. This is the committee that reviews the safety of pesticides such as glyphosate. It is a huge conflict of interest that representatives of organizations with direct or indirect economic interests from the sales or use of pesticides should be allowed to make the decisions on whether these products should be restricted or banned. This really is a case of the foxes being put in charge of the hen house.[16]

The conclusion by EFSA that glyphosate was unlikely to cause cancer raised serious concerns with numerous international and European researchers and scientists. Given the substantial studies and the clear and transparent analysis by IARC to give glyphosate a 2A rating for cancer, the decision by BfR did not seem credible. Consequently, ninety-six professors, independent academics, and governmental scientists from around the world sent an open letter to Mr. Vytenis Andriukaitis, commissioner of health and food safety, European Commission, criticizing the methodologies and decision-making procedures of the BfR. They wrote, "We have banded together and write to you at this time to express our deep concern over the recent European Food Safety Agency (EFSA) decision that the widely used herbicide, glyphosate 'is unlikely to pose a carcinogenic hazard to humans.' "

They explained that they did not find BfR decision credible because scientific evidence did not support their conclusions, and the organization was not transparent about how it came to its decision. "Accordingly, we urge you and the European Commission to disregard the flawed EFSA finding on glyphosate in your formulation of glyphosate health and environmental policy for Europe and to call for a transparent, open and credible review of the scientific literature."[17]

EXAMPLES OF REGULATORY INACTION, NEGLECT, AND MISMANAGEMENT

Pesticides are used in our food production because they are toxic. Their primary role is to kill pests, diseases, and weeds by poisoning them. Regulatory authorities have a duty to ensure that humans and the environment are not being adversely affected by these poisons. This duty of care is particularly important when it comes to protecting the health of our children—our future.

So far it has been the actions of civil society and concerned scientists that have made regulators take limited actions on the uses of some chemicals. Their intervention can sometimes result in modifications in how the chemicals are used or, in rare cases, a ban to improve the safety of humans and the environment. It should not be up to the public to spend enormous human and financial resources to prove that they are harmful. It should be up to the industry, the sector that profits from these chemicals, to prove unequivocally that they are safe when people and the environment are exposed to them.

Regulatory authorities should take a preventive approach as advocated by the USPCP. When a newly published peer-reviewed scientific study indicates a health issue with the current use patterns of a pesticide, the precautionary principle* should be invoked to ensure that there is no harm. This could mean that the use of the chemical be suspended until independently published, peer-reviewed scientific testing shows what level of exposure is safe.

Unfortunately the opposite approach is the reality, with regulatory authorities ignoring the new science and usually only taking limited action after years of work by the concerned sections of civil society and the scientific community.

GLYPHOSATE REGULATION—DECADES OF IGNORING SCIENTIFIC RESEARCH

The regulation of glyphosate is a good example of authorities ignoring an extensive body of published scientific study showing the harm that can be caused by this widely used pesticide. According to Monsanto, it is the most common herbicide used in the world, and its use is increasing due to the introduction of glyphosate-resistant GMO crops.

Glyphosate and its formulations are considered safe, so consequently they are widely used to spray roadsides, sidewalks, children's playgrounds, parks, and gardens as well as in food production. Commonly cited information arguing that glyphosate is very safe is found on the website for EXTOXNET, The Extension Toxicology Network. EXTOXNET is gradually being replaced by fact

---

* The precautionary principle is used in policymaking when there is a suspected risk to the health of humans and the environment and states that under these circumstances it may not be necessary to wait for scientific certainty to take protective action.

sheets from the National Pesticide Information Center (NPIC), a cooperative agreement between Oregon State University and the U.S. Environmental Protection Agency. The general fact sheet on glyphosate was reviewed in September 2010 and gives the impression that glyphosate-based products are very safe, though they may cause some problems "at very high doses."[18] The fact sheet ignores the numerous studies showing that it causes numerous health problems at environmentally relevant levels.

CELL DAMAGE—PRECURSORS TO CANCER AND BIRTH DEFECTS

Research has shown that glyphosate can cause genetic damage, developmental disruption, morbidity, and mortality even at what are currently considered normal levels of use.[19] The article "Differential Effects of Glyphosate and Roundup on Human Placental Cells and Aromatase," published by Richard et al. in *Environmental Health Perspectives*, revealed evidence that glyphosate damaged human placental cells within eighteen hours of exposure, even at concentrations lower than those found in commercially available pesticides and herbicides. The scientists stated that "this effect increases with concentration and time or in the presence of Roundup adjuvants."[20]

Researchers of a study published in the journal *Toxicology* studied four different commercial glyphosate formulations and observed breaks in 50 percent of the DNA strands in human liver cells at doses as low as five parts per million. This damage affects the way DNA sends messages to several physiological systems, including the endocrine system. The researchers stated that this is significant because the liver is the first detoxification organ and is sensitive to dietary pollutants.[21]

TERATOGENICITY (BIRTH DEFECTS) IN ANIMALS

Clements et al. published a study in 1997 showing damage to DNA in bullfrog tadpoles after exposure to glyphosate. The scientists concluded that glyphosate's "genotoxicity at relatively low concentrations" was of concern.[22] A 2003 study by Lajmanovich et al. found that up to 55 percent of tadpoles exposed to a glyphosate herbicide had deformities to the mouth, eyes, skull, vertebrae, and tails.[23] A 2003 study by Dallegrave et al. found that the offspring of pregnant rats dosed with glyphosate had increased skeletal abnormalities.[24]

A 2004 study conducted by biologists at Trent University, Carleton University (Canada), and the University of Victoria (Canada) showed that concentrations of several glyphosate herbicides at levels found in the environment caused developmental problems in tadpoles. The exposed tadpoles did not to grow to the normal size, took longer than normal to develop, and between 10 and 25 percent had abnormal sex organs.[25]

A 2010 study found that almost 60 percent of tadpoles treated with Roundup at one part per million had malformations such as kyphosis, scoliosis, and edema.[26] A 2012 study by Relyea found that tadpoles exposed to concentrations of Roundup found in the environment had changes to their tails.[27]

One of the most significant studies investigating the toxicity of both Roundup as a formulation and of glyphosate as the active ingredient, published by Alejandra Paganelli et al. in 2010, explains one of the ways they cause teratogenicity. The researchers found that both Roundup and glyphosate by itself caused severe malformations in the embryos of chickens and frogs and that this could occur in frogs when exposed to less than 0.5 parts per million. The researchers identified the specific mechanism that glyphosate and Roundup use to cause the malformations. They found that the chemicals disrupted a key biochemical mechanism, the retinoic acid signaling pathway.[28]

The retinoic acid signaling pathway is used by all vertebrates, including humans, to ensure the normal development of organs, bones and tissues in embryos. It is also essential for normal sexual development, especially in males. The pathway signals the exact time and place that the development of organs and tissues occurs in embryos. It also corrects malformations if they start. Disrupting its normal balance means that the various organs and tissues can be given signals to form incorrectly, and the pathway cannot correct any of these embryo malformations when they start forming.[29]

Research by Mesnage et al. found that Roundup from 1 ppm to 20,000 ppm causes cells of the human body to die through necrosis. At 50 ppm it delays the cellular apoptosis that is essential for the normal functioning and regeneration of cells, body tissues, and organs.[30] Delaying or stopping apoptosis is considered one of the causes of cancer.

GLYPHOSATE, CANCERS AND TUMORS

As stated previously in this chapter, the IARC classified glyphosate as the second-highest level of cancer causing substances based on several scientific studies showing that it causes a range of cancers. The following are examples of some of the many studies linking glyphosate to cancer.

A study conducted by Flower et al. 2004 examined the levels of cancer in the children of people who sprayed glyphosate for weed control. They found that these children had increased levels of all childhood cancers including all lymphomas such as non-Hodgkin's lymphoma.[31]

A case-controlled study published in March 1999 by Swedish scientists Lennart Hardell and Mikael Eriksson also linked non-Hodgkin's lymphoma (NHL) to exposure to a range of pesticides and herbicides, including glyphosate.[32] Prior to the 1940s, non-Hodgkin's lymphoma was one of the world's rarest cancers. Now it is one of the most common. Between 1973 and 1991, the incidence of non-Hodgkin's lymphoma increased at the rate of 3.3 percent per year in the United States,

THE IARC CLASSIFIED GLYPHOSATE
as the second–highest level of cancer causing substances based on several scientific studies showing that it causes a range of cancers.

making it the third fastest-growing cancer.[33] In Sweden, the incidence of NHL has increased at the rate of 3.6 percent per year in men and 2.9 percent per year in women since 1958.

Several animal studies have shown that glyphosate can cause gene mutations and chromosomal aberrations. These types of genetic damage can be the precursors of cancer.[34]

A study published in 2004 found that glyphosate-based herbicides caused cell-cycle dysregulation, which leads to cancers. According to the researchers, "Cell-cycle dysregulation is a hallmark of tumor cells and human cancers. Failure in the cell-cycle checkpoints leads to genomic instability and subsequent development of cancers from the initial affected cell." The researchers tested several glyphosate-based pesticides and found that all of them caused cell-cycle dysregulation.[35] Glyphosate has also been shown to cause oxidative stress, one of the hallmarks of cancer.[36]

Research (mentioned previously in chapters 1 and 2) published in the peer-reviewed scientific journal *Food and Chemical Toxicology* in 2013 found that glyphosate at residue levels commonly found in people caused a five- to thirteenfold increase in the multiplication of estrogen-sensitive human breast cancer cells.[37]

The only published, peer-reviewed, lifetime comparison feeding study found that rats fed a diet that contains a proportion of GM maize or minute residues of Roundup had significantly higher rates of tumors, kidney disease, liver damage, and other negative health effects.

Females that were fed either GM maize or non-GM maize with minute roundup residues developed large mammary tumours almost always more often than and sooner than the controls. All the non-control females, except for one that had an ovarian tumor, had mammary hypertrophies (enlarged mammary glands) and in some cases hyperplasia with atypia (nodules in the mammary glands). Treated males presented four times the number of tumors that were large enough to be felt by hand than the controls, and these occurred up to six hundred days earlier.[38]

ENDOCRINE DISRUPTION
Thongprakaisang et al. found glyphosate acted like estrogen to cause the multiplication of estrogen-sensitive breast cancer cells.[39]

Gasnier et al. in 2009 reported endocrine-disrupting actions of glyphosate at 0.5 ppm. According to the authors this is "800 times lower than the level authorized in some food or feed (400 ppm, USEPA, 1998)."[40]

Professor Séralini's 2014 study published in *Environmental Sciences Europe* found that both GM maize and Roundup act as endocrine disrupters and their consumption resulted in female rats dying —at a rate two to three times higher than the control animals. The pituitary gland was the second most disabled organ and the sex hormonal balance was modified in females fed with the GMO and Roundup treatments.[41] Quite a bit of controversy surrounded this particular study, which I will discuss in more detail in the final chapter.

DISRUPTION OF METABOLIC PATHWAYS

One of the most significant studies was published by Samsel and Seneff in the peer-reviewed scientific journal *Entropy* in 2013. This comprehensive review, titled "Glyphosate's Suppression of Cytochrome P450 Enzymes and Amino Acid Biosynthesis by the Gut Microbiome: Pathways to Modern Diseases," showed how glyphosate disrupted numerous biochemical pathways within the human body, including gut microorganisms, and consequently could lead to numerous diseases.[42] The evidence in the scientific paper is voluminous and compelling and opens up significant areas where research is needed on glyphosate and other chemicals' potential to adversely affect human health.

Cytochrome P450 (CYP) is known as a superfamily of enzymes that are responsible for around 75 percent of metabolic reactions involved in drug metabolism and the oxidation of organic molecules and are present in most tissues of the body. They metabolize thousands of chemicals made by the body and those absorbed from external sources such as foods, water, gut microorganisms, and the atmosphere. They are also involved in the metabolism and synthesis of numerous key biochemical compounds such as retinol, vitamin D, neurotransmitters such as serotonin and melatonin, and other compounds critical to health such as L-tryptophan and cholesterol. CYPs are very important in synthesis and metabolism of hormones such as estrogen, testosterone, aldosterone, androstenedione, cortisol, corticosterone, and dehydroepiandrosterone to ensure homeostasis. Very significantly CYPs metabolize toxic compounds such as pesticides, drugs, and other chemicals

Samsel and Seneff identified numerous ways that glyphosate disrupts the CYP enzymes and how this can cause many diseases. The authors state:

> Glyphosate's inhibition of cytochrome P450 (CYP) enzymes is an overlooked component of its toxicity to animals. CYP enzymes play crucial roles in biology, one of which is to detoxify xenobiotics. Thus, glyphosate enhances the damaging effects of other food borne chemical residues and environmental toxins. Negative impact on the body is insidious and manifests slowly over time as inflammation damages cellular systems throughout the body. Here, we show how interference with CYP enzymes acts synergistically with disruption of the biosynthesis of aromatic amino acids by gut bacteria, as well as impairment in serum sulfate transport. Consequences are most of the diseases and conditions associated with a Western diet, which include gastrointestinal disorders, obesity, diabetes, heart disease, depression, autism, infertility, cancer, and Alzheimer's disease. We explain the documented effects of glyphosate and its ability to induce disease, and we show that glyphosate is the "textbook example" of exogenous semiotic entropy: the disruption of homeostasis by environmental toxins.[43]

Samsel and Seneff's research also confirms the earlier research by Paganelli et al. on glyphosate's ability to disrupt the retinoic acid pathway. As stated previously, retinoic acid has a key role in the development of embryos to stop birth defects (teratogenicity) from developing. One of the ways it does this is to metabolize excess retinol (a form of vitamin A). A key enzyme in retinoic acid pathway that does this is CYP26, one of the many members of the cytochrome P450 superfamily. The ability of glyphosate to disrupt this important group of enzymes is an example of one of the ways it disturbs the retinoic acid pathway.

The potential of numerous other chemicals, including pesticides, to adversely affect the cytochrome P450 pathways in all living biota, including humans, needs to be actively researched given that these pathways are responsible for a significant percentage of metabolic functions. At this stage research is in its infancy, and the complexity of these interactions is not adequately understood due to being mostly overlooked. The body of evidence presented by Samsel and Seneff shows that disruption of these key metabolic systems by xenobiotics such as synthetic chemicals is one of the reasons for the dramatic increases of a large range of diseases, especially in developed countries and the growing middle classes in developing countries.

This finding is reinforced by the significant number of studies documenting a range of birth defects, cancers, and other diseases linked to the exposure of glyphosate.

DISRUPTION OF THE GUT MICROBIOME
Samsel and Seneff's paper identified how glyphosate disrupted the gut microbiome, causing the suppression of biosynthesis of cytochrome P450 enzymes and key amino acids. In a later paper, "Glyphosate, Pathways to Modern Diseases II: Celiac Sprue and Gluten Intolerance," Samsel and Seneff showed how the current increase in celiac disease and gluten intolerance in people was linked to glyphosate's adverse effects on the gut microbiome. They highlighted that glyphosate is patented as a biocide, and consequently it kills the beneficial gut bacteria, leading to a rise in intestinal diseases.[44] Krüger et al. showed that glyphosate has this effect in the microbiome of horses and cows.[45] Shehata et al. found the same effects in poultry; the researchers state, "Highly pathogenic bacteria such as *Salmonella* Entritidis, *Salmonella* Gallinarum, *Salmonella* Typhimurium, *Clostridium perfringens* and *Clostridium botulinum* are highly resistant to glyphosate. However, most of the beneficial bacteria such as *Enterococcus faecalis*, *Enterococcus faecium*, *Bacillus*

badius, *Bifidobacterium adolescentis* and *Lactobacillus* spp. were found to be moderate to highly susceptible."[46] Both groups of researchers postulated that glyphosate is associated with the increase in botulism-mediated diseases in these domestic farm animals.

KIDNEY AND LIVER DISEASE

Since the 1990s, researchers in Sri Lanka have reported an epidemic of kidney failure in rice paddy workers exposed to glyphosate in combination with minerals in hard water. According to Jayasumana et al., glyphosate's strong chelating properties allow it to combine with heavy metals and arsenic in hard waters, resulting in damage to renal tissues and thereby causing chronic kidney diseases. The authors concluded that, "The GMA [glyphosate-metal/arsenic complex] lattice hypothesis gives rational and consistent explanations to the many observations and unanswered questions associated with the mysterious kidney disease in rural Sri Lanka. Furthermore, it may explain the similar epidemics of CKDu [chronic kidney disease of unknown etiology] observed in Andra Pradesh, India and Central America."[47]

> **SINCE THE 1990s**, *researchers in Sri Lanka have reported an epidemic of kidney failure in rice paddy workers exposed to glyphosate in combination with minerals in hard water.*

In the lifetime feeding study of rats conducted by Séralini et al. in 2014, the treated males displayed liver congestions and necrosis at rates 2.5 to 5.5 times higher than the controls, as well as marked and severe kidney nephropathies (kidney damage) at rates generally 1.3 to 2.3 greater than the controls.

In a later published study designed to understand why Roundup and glyphosate-based herbicides caused the kidney and liver damage in rats, scientists discovered that ultra-low doses of the herbicides disrupted the functions of numerous genes, which resulted in changes consistent with multiple kidney and liver disease problems.

The researchers stated, "Our results suggest that chronic exposure to a GBH (glyphosate-based herbicide) in an established laboratory animal toxicity model system at an ultra-low, environmental dose can result in liver and kidney damage with potential significant health implications for animal and human populations."[48]

OXIDATIVE STRESS AND CELL DAMAGE

Oxidative stress is an imbalance between free radicals and the body's ability to repair the damage caused by free radicals. It is one of the hallmarks of cancer and a contributing factor to many chronic diseases, having been linked to Alzheimer's, cancer, and Parkinson's disease, among other health issues. Cattani et al. found that both acute and chronic exposure to Roundup induced oxidative stress resulting in neural cell death and neurotoxic effects in the hippocampus region of the brain in immature rats.[49] Lushchak et al. found that a ninety-six-hour exposure to low levels of Roundup in water caused oxidative stress to the cells in the brains, livers, and kidneys of goldfish.[50] Studies by El-Shenawy and de Liz Oliveira Cavalli et al. confirm that Roundup and glyphosate caused oxidative stress and necrosis in cells, including the liver, testis, and Sertoli cells in rats.[51]

DEVELOPMENTAL NEUROTOXICITY

Developmental neurotoxicity is where a chemical interferes with the normal development of nerve cells. A study mentioned in the 1st Chapter that was published in the scientific journal NeuroToxicology, shows that nerve cells do not develop properly when exposed to small amounts of glyphosate. The researchers show how glyphosate exposed cells had shorter and unbranched axons as well less complex dendritic arbors.[52]

GLYPHOSATE LINKED TO TWENTY–TWO DISEASES IN THE UNITED STATES

Research conducted by Dr. Nancy Swanson and colleagues shows a link between the increase in the use of glyphosate, the acres of

NUMBER OF CHILDREN (6–21 YRS) WITH
AUTISM SERVED BY IDEA

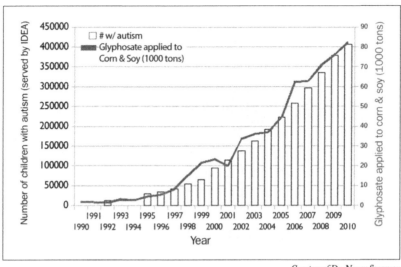

Courtesy of Dr. Nancy Swanson

DEATHS DUE TO THYROID CANCER (ICD C93 &193)

Plotted against %GE corn & soy (R=0.876, p<=7.947e-05) and glyphosate applied
to corn & soy (R=0.9583, p<=2.082e-08)

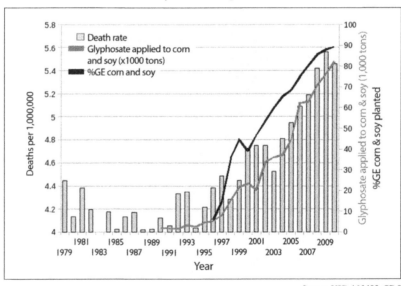

Sources: USDA:NASS; CDC

AGE ADJUSTED DEATHS DUE TO OBESITY (ICD E66 & 278)

Plotted against %GE corn & soy (R=0.9618, p<=3.504e-06) and glyphosate
applied to corn & soy (R=0.9616, p<=1.695e-08)

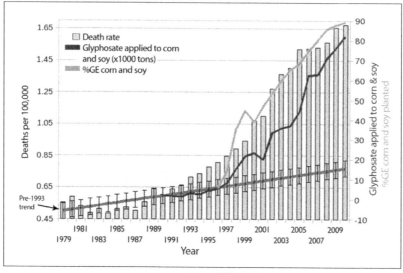

Sources: USDA:NASS; CDC, Courtesy of Dr. Nancy Swanson

DEATHS FROM ALZHEIMER'S (ICD G30.9 & 331.0)

Plotted against glyphosate use (R=0.9319, p<=9.903e-08) and
%GE corn & soy (R=0.9511, p<=5.51e-06)

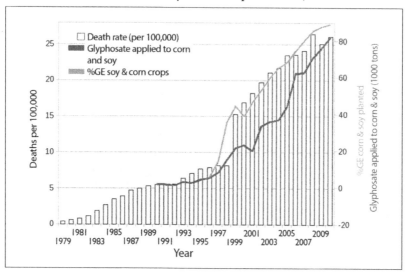

Sources: USDA:NASS; CDC, Courtesy of Dr. Nancy Swanson

ANNUAL INCIDENCE OF DIABETES (AGE ADJUSTED)

Plotted against %GE corn & soy crops planted (R=0.9547, p<=1.978e-06) along with glyphosate applied to corn & soy in U.S. (R=0.935, p<=8.303e-08).

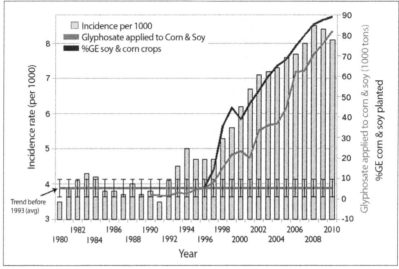

Sources: USDA: NASS; CDC, Courtesy of Dr. Nancy Swanson

URINARY/BLADDER CANCER INCIDENCE (AGE ADJUSTED)

Plotted against % GE corn and soy (R=0.9449, p<=7.1e-06) and glyphosate applied to corn and soy (R=0.981, p<=4.702e-09)

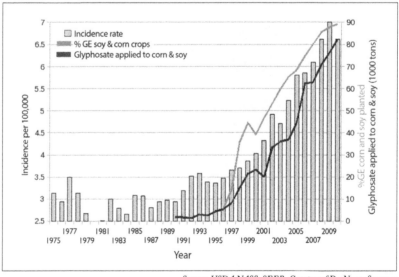

Sources: USDA:NASS; SEER, Courtesy of Dr. Nancy Swanson

DEATHS DUE TO MULTIPLE SCLEROSIS (ICD G35 & 340)

Plotted against percentage of GE soy & corn (R=0.9477, p<=6.339e-06) and glyphosate applied to soy & corn (R=0.9005, p<=5.079e-07)

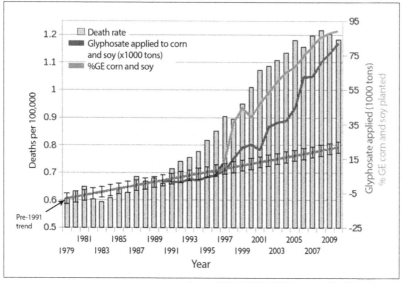

Sources: USDA:NASS; CDC, Courtesy of Dr. Nancy Swanson

DEATHS DUE TO INTESTINAL INFECTION
(ICD A04, A09; 004, 009)

Plotted against glyphosate applied to corn and soy (R=0.9762, p<=6.494e-09)

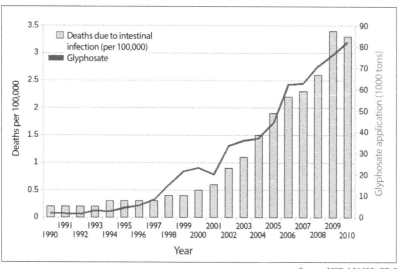

Sources: USDA:NASS; CDC

LIVER AND INTRAHEPATIC BILE DUCT CANCER
INCIDENCE (AGE ADJUSTED)

Plotted against glyphosate applied to corn & soy (R=0.9596, p<=4.624e-08) along
with %GE corn & soy planted in U.S. (R=0.9107, p<=5.402e-05)

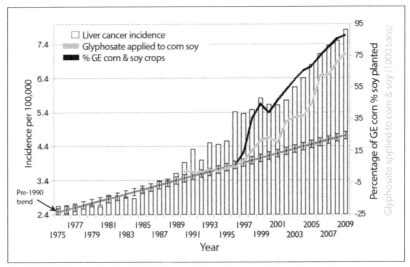

Sources: USDA:NASS; SEER

land under GMOs, and twenty-two diseases prevalent in the United States.[53]

Dr. Swanson used statistical data from credible sources such as the CDC and USDA and created graphs to show the correlations. The data was analyzed by using a standard statistical method called the Pearson's correlation coefficients. The Pearson's correlation coefficients show a less than one chance in ten thousand ($< 10^{-5}$) that the increase in glyphosate applications and the increase in the twenty diseases is a coincidence. The data shows a very strong probability that glyphosate is linked to the increase in hypertension, diabetes, obesity, Alzheimer's, senile dementia, autism, inflammatory bowel disease, intestinal infections, end-stage renal disease, acute kidney failure, and cancers of the thyroid, liver, bladder, pancreas, and kidney.

The graphs show sudden increases in the rates of diseases starting in the mid-1990s. These changes coincide with the commercial production of GMO crops, particularly the glyphosate-resistant crops. Since the mid-1990s, no other pesticide has increased in use as much as glyphosate, thanks to the expansion of glyphosate-resistant genetically engineered crops.

While correlation is not proof of causation, the Pearson's correlation coefficient, along with the numerous scientific studies linking glyphosate to a range of diseases, presents a strong body of evidence that glyphosate regulation is seriously inadequate in protecting human health.

GLYPHOSATE INTERFERES WITH KEY PROTEIN SYNTHESIS

Anthony Samsel and Stephanie Seneff published a review of research literature showing that glyphosate is a synthetic amino acid and analogue of glycine — one of the fundamental amino acids in all living species, including humans. Glycine has numerous roles in the human body including DNA, protein synthesis, hormones and many other key metabolic roles. The researchers showed evidence how the substation of glyphosate for glycine is major factor in the epidemic of non-communicable diseases.

"Glyphosate substitution for conserved glycines can easily explain a link with diabetes, obesity, asthma, chronic obstructive pulmonary disease (COPD), pulmonary edema, adrenal insufficiency, hypothyroidism, Alzheimer's disease, amyotrophic lateral sclerosis (ALS), Parkinson's disease, prion diseases, lupus, mitochondrial disease, non- Hodgkin's lymphoma, neural tube defects, infertility, hypertension, glaucoma, osteoporosis, fatty liver disease and kidney failure. The correlation data together with the direct biological evidence make a compelling case for glyphosate action as a glycine analogue to account for much of glyphosate's toxicity."[54]

REGULATORY RESPONSES NOT CONSISTENT WITH THE PUBLISHED SCIENCE

The U.S. EPA and the EFSA recent decision to significantly increase the allowed MRLs and ADIs of glyphosate in food and other crops in response to a petition prepared by Monsanto, despite the large number of peer-reviewed studies showing multiple health problems associated with exposure to glyphosate, was a grave disappointment to many. Unfortunately, it should not come as a surprise, as Dr. Colborn stated, "The U.S. EPA has rarely used the open literature in its risk assessments, generally using only data submitted by manufacturers."[55]

Monsanto petitioned for the MRL increase because the combination of glyphosate-tolerant GMO crops and using glyphosate to quickly desiccate crops like wheat, has resulted in a major increase in the amount of glyphosate used in farming. As a result, there were more opportunities for glyphosate residues to exceed the existing MRLs. Rather than risking farmers finding a way to reduce the glyphosate usage in agriculture in accordance with the law and possibly losing sales, Monsanto sought to change the law by increasing these MRLs so that testing will show that glyphosate residues are below the MRLs and therefore being used "safely."

EUROPEAN REGULATORS AND GLYPHOSATE

In general, the countries of the European Union tend to review pesticides more frequently than other countries in the world. To their credit, they have banned or restricted more pesticides than other regions, but the way some of these reviews are conducted needs to be seriously questioned.

Specific countries in the EU are responsible for testing specific pesticides. In the case of glyphosate, Germany is the designated country, and it is given the title of the rapporteur member state to carry out this research. Germany's Federal Institute for Risk Assessment (BfR) has been given the responsibility of testing glyphosate.

According to Swanson and Ho the BfR used a document prepared by a pesticide industry organization called the Glyphosate Task Force (GTF) composed of various European Chemical Companies and Monsanto, as the basis of their review.

They reported that "The rapporteur member state (RMS) has accepted, without question, virtually all of the unpublished reports given to them by the chemical companies. Much of the information is blacked out (author, report title, laboratory) but the sponsoring company is named (Monsanto, Syngenta etc.) and the reports are referred to by a number."

Swanson and Ho described how the GTF used only data from the least toxic industry studies, relegating conflicting data to "supplementary status." The GTF rejected all the studies that tested complete formulations, even though only formulations are used in farming and food production, and accepted only studies based on 99 percent pure glyphosate. However, the glyphosate used in farming comes from industrial processes that do not reach those levels of purity and contains various toxic by-products and metabolites. Although the public uses only formulations, like Roundup, studies testing Roundup itself were rejected by the task force!

The GTF rejected the overwhelming majority of independent peer-reviewed studies so they could ignore the extensive body of scientific evidence showing the harm caused by glyphosate.

> **THE GTF ALSO REJECTED** *all the human studies, even though several of these were considered relevant by the IARC panel when they classified glyphosate as a probable human carcinogen.*

The GTF took all of the peer-reviewed studies and proceeded to find excuses to throw out the ones that didn't agree with the already-accepted industry studies. First they threw out all studies that used the actual product (Roundup, Rodeo, Lasso, etc.) because the active ingredient percentage is not the same from product to product and the surfactants used vary from product to product so the results cannot be compared and are thus inconclusive. They threw out any studies where they deemed that the dosage was unreasonably high, compared to their "safe" levels, although their own toxicology studies showed the same results at the higher dosages. They threw out any that they decided were inapplicable to mammals (frog embryos, insect larvae, etc.) or that were administered in a non-natural way (injection). They took issue with how many rats/mice/dogs/guinea pigs were or were not used and how things were or were not measured or reported.

The GTF also rejected all the human studies, even though several of these were considered relevant by the IARC panel when they classified glyphosate as a probable human carcinogen.

The greatest concern is that the EU regulator accepted the document submitted by the pesticide industry and dismissed the huge body of independent scientific evidence. Just as Vallianatos stated about the U.S. EPA, the German BfR stands accused of "plagiarizing industry studies and cutting and pasting the findings of industry as their own."[56]

Regulators' reaction to the Paganelli study, which found that glyphosate caused severe malformations in the embryos of chickens and frogs, also provides a good insight into how some of the review processes work.

The regulators and the pesticide industry strongly rebutted the Paganelli et al. study rather than trying to repeat it to see if they could get the same results, even though repeating a scientific study by following its material and methods is regarded as the correct way to check the results for accuracy and consistency. The German Federal Office of Consumer Protection and Food Safety (BVL) produced a rebuttal document using other studies to invalidate the Paganelli study, claiming there was no evidence that glyphosate causes birth defects, a move that raises concerns about how regulators and the pesticide industry work together to ensure that toxic products are still sold and widely used despite a strong body of science showing these products should be severely restricted or banned. The regulators' assessment minimized the evidence presented by Paganelli et al., claiming that the exposure conditions used by the researchers were "highly artificial" and that there was "no clear-cut link" between birth defects and heavy pesticide use.[57]

In response, Michael Antoniou and a team of researchers published a study in the journal of *Environmental and Analytical Toxicology* in 2012 subtitled "Divergence of Regulatory Decisions from

Scientific Evidence," documenting how the German Federal Office of Consumer Protection and Food Safety (BVL) not only ignored an extensive body of published science, they actively misrepresented the data in the selective studies they used to set the acceptable daily intake.[58] The independent scientists who reviewed the studies used by BVL found that there was more evidence that glyphosate caused malformations, not less as stated by the German regulators. The independent scientists concluded:

> However, examination of the German authorities' draft assessment report on the industry studies, which underlies glyphosate's EU authorisation, revealed further evidence of glyphosate's teratogenicity [ability to cause birth defects]. Many of the malformations found were of the type defined in the scientific literature as associated with retinoic acid teratogenesis. Nevertheless, the German and EU authorities minimized these findings in their assessment and set a potentially unsafe acceptable daily intake (ADI) level for glyphosate.[59]

Antoniou et al. concluded that there was a need for a new review of the data by independent scientists to ensure a credible regulatory decision that will guarantee that people do not suffer adverse health effects from the permitted uses of glyphosate.[60]

UNPUBLISHED INDUSTRY–SPONSORED STUDIES

The German authorities' rebuttal of the Paganelli et al. study and their decision to approve the renewal of glyphosate increasing the MRLs and ADIs raises the issue of the use of unpublished non-peer-reviewed, industry-sponsored studies by regulatory authorities. The BVL's negations relied partly on unpublished industry studies commissioned for regulatory purposes. These studies made the claim that glyphosate did not cause birth defects or act as a reproductive toxin.

Regulatory authorities tend to use these studies to make their assessments instead of peer-reviewed studies that are published in scientific journals.

A high proportion of these unpublished industry studies are not available for review and assessments by other scientists and stakeholders because they are regarded as commercial-in-confidence. In many cases the reports and the toxicological data can only be obtained through court cases and/or the relevant discovery and freedom of information legislations in their respective countries.

This was the case with the review of the German authority's assessment of glyphosate by Antoniou et al. While the scientists managed to obtain the assessment report on glyphosate that the German authorities compiled in 1998, the industry toxicological data that was summarized in the assessment report was not publicly available. This data was claimed to be commercially confidential by the chemical company. In order to get this data the Pesticide Action Network Europe took legal action through the courts.[61]

Another example of this is a paper that was published by Monsanto in the journal *Critical Reviews in Toxicology* in March 2015, the same month IARC published its statements that glyphosate caused cancer in animals and was a probable human carcinogen. Monsanto's paper concluded that the studies it reviewed "support the conclusion that glyphosate does not present concern with respect to carcinogenic potential in humans."[62]

Unlike the IARC monograph that was open, transparent, and detailed, all the studies and the experts' conclusions, the Monsanto paper used commercial in confidence studies, which are not available for the public and other researchers to examine. The authors of the Monsanto paper stated, "Most toxicological studies informing regulatory evaluations are of commercial interest and are proprietary in nature. Given the widespread attention to this molecule, the authors gained access to carcinogenicity data submitted to regulatory agencies and present overviews of each study, followed by a weight of evidence evaluation of tumor incidence data."

The credibility of all regulatory decisions will continue to be questioned because they can never be considered open and transparent, while the studies they use are hidden from the public, researchers, and experts to review and evaluate the decisions. The use of unpublished, hidden industry studies is a gross conflict of interest, and the question that we all have to ask is: What are they trying to hide from us? This will contribute to the lack of trust by the public and many in the scientific community about regulatory decisions and the competence of authorities to make these decisions.

REACH—THE EUROPEAN UNION'S COMPREHENSIVE REVIEW OF CHEMICALS

The European Union (EU) has started a major review of all widely used chemicals under a new regulation called the Registration, Evaluation, and Authorization of Chemicals (REACH).[63]

REACH started in 2007 and will be fully implemented by 2018. Initially, their assessments were based on chemicals produced or imported in the EU at more than 1,000 metric tons per year. By 2018 it will cover chemicals that are in the order of one metric ton per year. About 143,000 chemical substances marketed in the European Union were pre-registered by the December 1, 2008 deadline.[64]

REACH will be missing many key tests, such as those for cocktails of chemicals; the special requirements of fetuses, newborns, and growing children; endocrine disruption; pesticide metabolites; intergenerational effects; epigenetic changes and developmental neurotoxicity. It will also allow products that are produced in the EU or imported in quantities of less than one metric ton to be exempt.

REACH is considered to be a good start in that this will be the first time in the world that there has been a comprehensive review of all the common chemicals that are used in a region. It will be the first time that regulatory bodies will assess formulated products for their adverse effects instead of assessing only single active ingredients.

REGULATORY AUTHORITIES *using hidden, unpublished, non-peer-reviewed, industry-sponsored studies should be seen as a major problem in the current regulatory decision-making processes.*

Instead of congratulating the EU for taking such a long overdue and important initiative and following the EU's example, a group of countries—including the United States, Brazil, Australia, India, Japan, Mexico, Singapore, South Africa, Thailand, Chile, Israel, South Korea, and Malaysia—put diplomatic pressure on the EU to water down the regulation on the basis that it would hamper the free trade in chemicals.

However, given the way EFSA has reviewed glyphosate and other chemicals in the past, many of those concerned about chemical regulation have very little confidence in the REACH process. They doubt that the decisions will protect people, children, and the environment from harm and see this as an expensive public relations exercise rather than a transparent and competent regulatory process that will deliver satisfactory outcomes.

THE NEED FOR TRANSPARENT, PUBLISHED, PEER-REVIEWED SCIENCE

Regulatory authorities using hidden, unpublished, non-peer-reviewed, industry-sponsored studies should be seen as a major problem in the current regulatory decision-making processes. As well as the issue of conflicts of interest, there is also the fact that the public has the right to know about the research used to determine the safety of the pesticides regularly found in their food.

Good science is based on peer-reviewed papers that are published in credible journals. These papers should clearly document the materials and methods used so that other scientists can accurately repeat the research to see if they can consistently get the same results. This will confirm the veracity and the credibility of the research.

These papers should be reviewed by independent experts in the field for an unbiased and critical analysis of the research. One of the purposes of peer review is to ensure that the researchers have not overlooked any aspects in the design of experiments and the interpretation of data that may have influenced the outcomes of the research and the resulting conclusions. Studies published in peer-reviewed journals are available for all the relevant stakeholders to read and analyze, which ensures that the process is transparent and allows a wider and more critical debate over the data and conclusions.

Involved researchers should also declare any potential conflict of interest, such as if they are paid by the industry to do the study. This transparency helps to overcome the issue of hidden agendas and bias and should be seen as an essential part of a fully open process. There is a lot of literature documenting or alleging that the industry has manipulated data to ensure favorable regulatory outcomes. Removing the secrecy and ensuring that all the decisions are made on the basis of the transparent processes that come with published peer-reviewed studies will reduce, if not eliminate, allegations of industry bias and interference. Unfortunately this is not the case with the current practices.

INCONSISTENCIES OF VARIOUS REGULATORY AUTHORITIES

Another important reason for ensuring that regulatory decisions are made on the basis of published, peer-review science is to remove the many inconsistencies in the decisions made by regulatory authorities. It's senseless that the residue levels of chemical formulas that one country deems unsafe for use, another country deems safe and legal, even though what's dangerous for humans in one country should be just as dangerous elsewhere.

Chlorpyrifos has been banned from use in the production of food in the United States, but most countries have ignored the scientific studies and continue to allow its widespread use. DDT is still widely used in countries like India, China, and Uganda, despite the overwhelming body of scientific evidence indicating the numerous health and environmental problems that it causes and despite the fact that there are numerous safer alternatives.

Atrazine is one of the most commonly used herbicides globally; however, it was banned in the European Union and Switzerland because it had polluted most water sources, was detected in a substantial percentage of rain samples, and caused a wide range of negative health effects.

The Australian regulatory processes are good examples of these inconsistencies. A review published by the World Wildlife Fund and the National Toxics Network showed that Australian farmers use around eighty chemicals that were banned in other countries because they pose risks to human health and the environment. The authors state, "The list includes 17 chemicals that are known, likely or probable carcinogens, and 48 chemicals flagged as having the potential to interfere with hormones. More than 20 have been classified as either extremely or highly hazardous by the World Health Organization yet remain available for use on Australian farms."[65]

Australia is usually among the last countries in the world to ban toxic chemicals, sometimes decades after publication of peer-reviewed science that other countries used as the basis to withdraw these chemicals from food production. Endosulfan is a good example. Australia was one of the last countries in the world to withdraw it from use. Also, when the U.S. EPA ended all food uses of chlorpyrifos after studies linked it to a range of negative health outcomes, the Australian regulator decided that there was no need to act on these studies and make similar changes to the way chlorpyrifos is used.

These inconsistencies show that the current processes of making regulatory decisions are more about political debates rather than logical decisions made on credible published science. They also confirm that the basis of most regulatory decisions is a reactionary rather than precautionary approach to chemical regulation.

THE NEED FOR A NEW REGULATORY APPROACH

There is an overwhelming body of scientific and other evidence showing that the current pesticide regulatory systems are not sufficient to ensure that pesticide use is safe for humans and the environment.

The American Academy of Pediatrics "recommends that chemical-management policy in the United States be revised to protect children and pregnant women and to better protect other populations."[66]

The USPCP clearly states that regulatory agencies are failing in their responsibilities to prevent the public from contracting serious illnesses such as cancer from exposures to environmental toxins such as pesticides. "In large measure, adequate environmental health regulatory agencies and infrastructures already exist, but agencies responsible for promulgating and enforcing regulations related to environmental exposures are failing to carry out their responsibilities. . . . A precautionary, prevention-oriented approach should replace current reactionary approaches to environmental contaminants in which human harm must be proven before action is taken to reduce or eliminate exposure."[67]

Regulators are ignoring a huge body of credible, peer-reviewed scientific studies and are instead making most of their decisions based on unpublished industry studies. This approach is clearly flawed and strongly biased toward industry over independent scientists and researchers.

Dr. Theo Colborn wrote in *A Case for Revisiting the Safety of Pesticides*: "In conclusion, an entirely new approach to determine the safety of pesticides is needed. It is evident that contemporary acute and chronic toxicity studies are not protective of future generations. . . . To protect human health, however, a new regulatory approach is also needed that takes into consideration this vast new knowledge about the neurodevelopmental effects of pesticides, not allowing the uncertainty that accompanies scientific research to serve as an impediment to protective actions."[68]

Regulators need to remove all the conflicts of interests, such as using hidden, unpublished industry studies and allowing representatives from the chemical industries to be in positions of management and sit on the decision-making panels concerning their products. Until this is done, it is a myth that the regulators have "a rigorous, science-based, and transparent regulatory program for pesticides that continues to protect people's health and the environment."[69]

NOTES

[1] USDA 2013 Pesticide Data Program press release, http://www.usda.gov/wps/portal/usda/usdahome?contentid=2014/12/0276.xml.

[2] Dr. Vandana Shiva, Dr. Mira Shiva, and Dr. Vaibhav Singh, *Poisons in Our Food* (India: Natraj Publishers, 2012).

[3] Vallianatos, *Poison Spring.*

[4] American Academy of Pediatrics, *Chemical-Management Policy: Prioritizing Children's Health*, 2011 Policy Statement.

[5] Vallianatos, *Poison Spring.*

[6] Colborn, "A Case for Revisiting the Safety of Pesticides."

[7] Ibid.

[8] Bergman et al., *State of the Science of Endocrine Disrupting Chemicals 2012.*

[9] "U.S. President's Cancer Panel Annual Report," 2010.

[10] Dr. Nancy Swanson, Dr. Eva Sirinathsinghji, and Dr. Mae Wan Ho, "Scandal of Glyphosate Re-assessment in Europe, in Banishing Glyphosate," Institute of Science in Society, September 15, 2015, http://www.i-sis.org.uk/Banishing_Glyphosate.php.

[11] Stéphane Horel and Corporate Europe Observator, *Unhappy Meal: The European Food Safety Authority's Independence Problem*, October 2013, http://corporateeurope.org/sites/default/files/attachments/unhappy_meal_report_23_10_2013.pdf.

[12] Steven M. Druker, *Altered Genes, Twisted Truth: How the Venture to Genetically Engineer Our Food Has Subverted Science, Corrupted Government, and Systematically Deceived the Public* (Salt Lake City: Clear River Press, 2015).

[13] "Glyphosate," IARC Monographs–112.

[14] "SECOND Peer Review of Glyphosate," Office of Pesticides and Toxic Substances, United States Environmental Protection Agency, Washington, D.C., October 30, 1991.

[15] European Food Safety Authority, "Conclusion on the Peer Review of the Pesticide Risk Assessment of the Active Substance Glyphosate," *EFSA Journal* 13, no. 11 (2015): 4302; European Food Safety Authority, "Final Addendum to the Renewal Assessment Report," *EFSA Journal* 13, no. 11 (2015): 4302, http://registerofquestions.efsa.europa.eu/roqFrontend/outputLoader?output=ON-4302.

[16] S. Foucart, "Noire semaine pour l'espertise," *Le Monde* (Paris), 2015, http://www.lemonde.fr/acces-restreint/idees/article/2015/03/30/6d6b629b69676fc595686764649971_4605627_3232.html.

[17] Open Letter: Review of the Carcinogenicity of Glyphosate by EFSA and BfR, November 27, 2015, http://images.derstandard.at/2015/11/30/glyphosate.pdf.

[18] "Glyphosate General Fact Sheet," National Pesticide Information Center, September 2010, http://npic.orst.edu/factsheets/glyphogen.pdf (accessed January 26, 2014).

[19] Cox, "Glyphosate (Roundup)."

[20] Richard et al., "Differential Effects of Glyphosate and Roundup."

[21] Céline Gasnier et al., "Glyphosate-Based Herbicides are Toxic and Endocrine Disruptors in Human Cell Lines," *Toxicology* 262 (2009): 184–91.

[22] Chris Clements, Steven Ralph, and Michael Petras, "Genotoxicity of Select Herbicides in *Rana catesbeiana* Tadpoles Using the Alkaline Single-Cell Gel DNA Electrophoresis (Comet) Assay," *Environmental and Molecular Mutagenesis* 29, no. 3 (1997): 277–88.

[23] Rafael C. Lajmanovich, M. T. Sandoval, Paola M. Peltzer, "Induction of Mortality and Malformation in *Scinax nasicus* Tadpoles Exposed to Glyphosate Formulations," *Bulletin of Environmental Contamination Toxicology* 70, no. 3 (March 2003): 612–18.

[24] Eliane Dallegrave et al., "The Teratogenic Potential of the Herbicide Glyphosate-Roundup in Wistar Rats," *Toxicology Letters* 142, nos. 1–2 (April 2003): 45–52.

[25] Christina M. Howe et al., "Toxicity of Glyphosate-Based Pesticides to Four North American Frog Species," *Environmental Toxicology and Chemistry* 23, no. 8 (August 2004): 1928–38.

[26] Uthpala A. Jayawardena et al., "Toxicity of Agrochemicals to Common Hourglass Tree Frog (*Polypedates cruciger*) in Acute and Chronic Exposure," *International Journal of Agriculture and Biology* 12 (2010): 641–48.

[27] Rick A. Relyea, "New Effects of Roundup on Amphibians: Predators Reduce Herbicide Mortality; Herbicides Induce Antipredator Morphology," *Ecological Applications* 22 (2012): 634–47.

[28] Alejandra Paganelli et al., "Glyphosate-Based Herbicides Produce Teratogenic Effects on Vertebrates by Impairing Retinoic Acid Signaling," *Chemical Research in Toxicology* 23, no. 10 (August 2010): 1586–95.

[29] Ibid.

[30] Mesnage, Bernay, and Séralini, "Ethoxylated Adjuvants of Glyphosate-Based Herbicides."

[31] K. B. Flower, J. A. Hoppin, C. F. Lynch, A. Blair, C. Knott, D. L. Shore, et al., "Cancer Risk and Parental Pesticide Application in Children of Agricultural Health Study Participants," *Environmental Health Perspectives* 112, no. 5 (2004): 631–35.

[32] Lennart Hardell and Mikael Eriksson, "A Case-Control Study of Non-Hodgkin Lymphoma and Exposure to Pesticides," *Cancer* 85, no. 6 (March 15, 1999): 1353–60.

[33] Angela Harras, ed., *Cancer Rates and Risks*, 4th ed. (Washington, D.C.: U.S. Department of Health and Human Services, Public Health Service, National Institutes of Health, 1996).

[34] Cox, "Glyphosate (Roundup)."

[35] Julie Marc, Odile Mulner-Lorillon, and Robert Bellé, "Glyphosate-Based Pesticides Affect Cell Cycle Regulation," *Biology of the Cell* 96, no. 3 (April 2004): 245–49.

[36] W.H. Goodson, "Assessing the Carcinogenic Potential of Low-Dose Exposures to Chemical Mixtures in the Environment: The Challenge Ahead" *Carcinogenesis* 36, no. 1 (June 2015).

[37] Thongprakaisang et al., "Glyphosate Induces Human Breast Cancer Cells Growth."

[38] Gilles-Éric Séralini et al., "Long-Term Toxicity of a Roundup Herbicide and a Roundup-Tolerant Genetically Modified Maize, *Environmental Sciences Europe*, republished study (2014): 14.

[39] Thongprakaisang et al., "Glyphosate Induces Human Breast Cancer Cells Growth."

[40] Ibid.

[41] Séralini et al., "Long-Term Toxicity."

[42] Anthony Samsel and Stephanie Seneff, "Glyphosate's Suppression of Cytochrome P450 Enzymes and Amino Acid Biosynthesis by the Gut Microbiome: Pathways to Modern Diseases," *Entropy* 15, no. 4 (2013): 1416–63.

[43] Ibid.

[44] Anthony Samsel and Stephanie Seneff, "Glyphosate, Pathways to Modern Diseases II: Celiac Sprue and Gluten Intolerance," *Interdisciplinary Toxicology* 6, no. 4 (2013): 159–84, http://sustainablepulse.com/wp-content/uploads/2014/02/Glyphosate_II_Samsel-Seneff.pdf (accessed March 21, 2014).

[45] Monika Krüger, Awad Ali Shehata, Wieland Schrödl, and Arne Rodloff, "Glyphosate Suppresses the Antagonistic Effect of *Enterococcus* spp. on *Clostridium botulinum*," *Anaerobe* 20 (April 2013): 74–78.

[46] Awad Ali Shehata, Wieland Schrödl, Alaa A. Aldin, Hafez M. Hafez, and Monika Krüger, "The Effect of Glyphosate on Potential Pathogens and Beneficial Members of Poultry Microbiota in Vitro," *Current Microbiology* 66, no. 4 (2012): 350–58.

[47] Channa Jayasumana, Sarath Gunatilake, and Priyantha Senanayake, "Glyphosate, Hard Water and Nephrotoxic Metals: Are They the Culprits Behind the Epidemic of Chronic Kidney Disease of Unknown Etiology in Sri Lanka?," *International Journal of Environmental Research and Public Health* 11, no. 2 (February 2014): 2125–47.

[48] Robin Mesnage, Matthew Arno, Manuela Costanzo, Manuela Malatesta, Gilles-Éric Séralini, and Michael N. Antoniou, "Transcriptome Profile Analysis Reflects Rat Liver and Kidney Damage Following Chronic Ultra-Low Dose Roundup exposure," *Environmental Health* 14 (2015): 70.

[49] Daiane Cattani et al., "Mechanisms Underlying the Neurotoxicity Induced by Glyphosate-Based Herbicide in Immature Rat Hippocampus: Involvement of Glutamate Excitotoxicity," *Toxicology* 320 (March 2014): 34–45.

[50] Oleh V. Lushchak et al., "Low Toxic Herbicide Roundup Induces Mild Oxidative Stress in Goldfish Tissues," *Chemosphere* 76, no. 7 (2009): 932–37.

[51] Nahla S. El-Shenawy, "Oxidative Stress Responses of Rats Exposed to Roundup and Its Active Ingredient Glyphosate," *Environmental Toxicology and Pharmacology* 28,

no. 3 (November 2009): 379–85; Vera Lúcia de Liz Oliveira Cavalli et al., "Roundup Disrupted Male Reproductive Functions By Triggering Calcium-Mediated Cell Death In Rat Testis And Sertoli Cells," *Free Radical Biology & Medicine* 65 (December 2013): 335–46.

[52] Romina P. Coullery, María E. Ferrari, Silvana B. Rosso, Neuronal development and axon growth are altered by glyphosate through a WNT non-canonical signaling pathway, NeuroToxicology 52 (2016) 150–161

[53] Nancy Swanson, André Leu, Jon Abrahamson and Bradley Wallet, "Genetically Engineered Crops, Glyphosate and the Deterioration of Health in the United States of America," *Journal of Organic Systems* 9 (2014): 6–37.

[54] Anthony Samsel and Stephanie Seneff, Glyphosate pathways to modern diseases V: Amino acid analogue of glycine in diverse proteins, Journal of Biological Physics and Chemistry, Vol16, June 2016

[55] Colborn, "A Case for Revisiting the Safety of Pesticides."

[56] Swanson, Sirinathsinghji, and Ho, "Scandal of Glyphosate Re-assessment in Europe, in Banishing Glyphosate."

[57] German Federal Office of Consumer Protection and Food Safety regulators (BVL), http://www.powerbase.info/images/b/b8/BVL2010.comments.Paganelli.pdf.

[58] Michael Antoniou et al., "Teratogenic Effects of Glyphosate-Based Herbicides: Divergence of Regulatory Decisions from Scientific Evidence," *Journal of Environmental and Analytical Toxicology* (2012): S4:006. doi:10.4172/2161-0525.S4-006.

[59] Ibid.

[60] Ibid.

[61] Ibid.

[62] Helmut Greim, David Saltmiras, Volker Mostert, and Christian Strupp, "Evaluation of Carcinogenic Potential of the Herbicide Glyphosate, Drawing on Tumor Incidence Data from Fourteen Chronic/Carcinogenicity Rodent Studies," *Critical Reviews in Toxicology* 45, No. 3 (March 2015): 185–208.

[63] European Commission, "What is REACH?"

[64] Ibid.

[65] Jo Immig, "A List of Australia's Most Dangerous Pesticides," National Toxics Network, July 2010, http://www.ntn.org.au/wp/wp-content/uploads/2010/07/FINAL-A-list-of-Australias-most-dangerous-pesticides-v2.pdf.

[66] American Academy of Pediatrics, "Chemical-Management Policy: Prioritizing Children's Health," 2011 Policy Statement.

[67] "U.S. President's Cancer Panel Annual Report," 2010.

[68] Colborn, "A Case for Revisiting the Safety of Pesticides."

[69] USDA 2013 Pesticide Data Program press release.

MYTH 5

✖

"Pesticides are Essential to Farming"

"We will starve to death without pesticides."

The greatest of all the myths is that we must be exposed to numerous toxic chemicals; otherwise we will have mass starvation. This myth states that it is impossible to grow enough food without the widespread use of these poisons. Manufacturers, conventional farming organizations, and regulators consistently argue that not using these pesticides and other agrochemicals would cause crop failures and dramatic reductions in yields.

In fact the opposite is true.

Unless we radically change agriculture, the world will starve due to the unsustainable damage caused by current industrial agriculture systems to the environment and human health. The United Nations Millennium Ecosystem Assessment Synthesis Report is the most comprehensive study ever conducted into the state of the environment on the planet. This detailed report by many of the world's leading scientific experts showed that our current agricultural practices are clearly unsustainable: "Over the past 50 years, humans have changed ecosystems more rapidly and extensively than in any comparable period of time in human history, largely to meet rapidly growing demands for food, fresh water, timber, fiber, and fuel. This has resulted in a substantial and largely irreversible loss in the diversity of life on Earth."[1]

A 2001 study from the University of California stated that agriculture will be a major driver of global environmental change over the next fifty years, rivalling the effect of greenhouse gases in its impact. The lead author, David Tilman, found that the use of pesticides, chemical fertilizers, and habitat destruction have caused a major extinction event that is lowering the world's biodiversity and changing its ecology. Tilman stated, "Neither society nor most scientists understand the importance of agriculture. It's grossly misunderstood, barely on the radar screen, yet it is likely as important as climate change. We have to find wiser ways to farm."[2]

The International Assessment of Agricultural Knowledge, Science and Technology for Development (IAASTD) Synthesis Report is the largest review of our current global agricultural systems yet undertaken. This multi-stakeholder process involved over four hundred scientific authors, sixty-one countries, and a bureau co-sponsored by the United Nations Food and Agriculture Organization (FAO), the Global Environment Facility (GEF), United Nations Development Programme (UNDP), United Nations Environment Programme (UNEP), United Nations Educational, Scientific and Cultural Organization (UNESCO), the World Bank, and the World Health Organization (WHO).

The synthesis report found multiple environmental problems seriously affecting the sustainability of global agricultural production, including:

    I. *Land degradation and nutrient depletion:*
       a. Land degradation occurs on about 2,000 million ha of land worldwide affecting 38% of the world's cropland;
       b. has depleted soil nutrients, resulting in Nitrogen, Phosphorous and Potassium deficiencies covering 59%,

85%, and 90% of harvested area respectively in the year 2000;
c. coupled with a 1,136 million tonnes yr−1 loss of total global production;
d. 1.9 billion ha (and 2.6 billion people) today are affected by significant levels of land degradation.

II. *Salinity and acidification*:
a. Salinization affects about 10% of the world's irrigated land.

III. *Loss of biodiversity (above and below ground) and associated agroecological functions*:
a. Caused by repeated use of monoculture practices;
b. excessive use of agrichemicals;
c. agricultural expansion into fragile environments;
d. excessive land clearance of natural vegetation and as a result adversely affects productivity.

IV. *Reduced water availability, quality and access:*
a. Fifty years ago water withdrawal from rivers was one-third of what it is today.
b. Agriculture already consumes 70% of all global fresh-water withdrawn worldwide.

V. *Increasing pollution (air, water, land):*
a. Increasing pollution also contributes to water quality problems affecting rivers and streams.
b. There have also been negative impacts of pesticide and fertilizer use on soil, air and water resources throughout the world.
c. Agriculture contributes about 60% of anthropogenic emissions of CH_4 and about 50% of N_2O emissions.
d. Inappropriate fertilization has led to eutrophication and large dead zones in a number of coastal areas.
e. Inappropriate use of pesticides has lead to groundwater pollution, health problems and loss of biodiversity (IAASTD 2008).

The report stated, "The way the world grows its food will have to change radically to better serve the poor and hungry if the world is to cope with growing population and climate change while avoiding social breakdown and environmental collapse."

The IAASTD report did not endorse the GMO and industrial agriculture paradigms as solutions to improve sustainability, instead proposing to work at a more local level with lower inputs, family farms, and endorsed ecological farming methods, including organic farming.

The report concluded that our current agricultural production systems are unsustainable and need to change. "'Business as usual' is not an option if we want to achieve environmental sustainability."[3]

ORGANIC AGRICULTURE INCREASES BIODIVERSITY

Research shows that organic systems have the highest biodiversity in farm fields of any farming systems.

The largest biodiversity review of seventy-six studies from around the world comparing organic to conventional agriculture found that organic farming increases biodiversity at every level of the food chain, from soil biota such as bacteria to higher animals such as mammals.

> It identifies a wide range of taxa, including birds and mammals, invertebrates and arable flora that benefit from organic management through increases in abundance and/or species richness. It also highlights three broad management practices (prohibition/reduced use of chemical pesticides and inorganic fertilizers; sympathetic management of non-cropped habitats; and preservation of mixed farming) that are largely intrinsic (but not exclusive) to organic farming, and that are particularly beneficial for farmland wildlife.[4]

ORGANIC AGRICULTURE CAN HELP REVERSE CLIMATE CHANGE

Climate change is one of the greatest threats to biodiversity and the survival of many species, including our own. As parents, we have a responsibility to pass on a better world to our children and future generations. We don't want to be remembered as the generation that missed their window of opportunity and failed to stop climate change. A good body of peer-reviewed science clearly shows that not only does organic farming emit less greenhouse gases, because it captures CO_2 and stores it in the ground as soil organic matter, organic farming actually reduces greenhouse gas emissions.

Agriculture is directly and indirectly responsible for more than 50 percent of greenhouse gas emissions, depending on the boundaries and methodologies used to determine its emissions.[5]

A peer-reviewed scientific study of the Rodale Farming Systems Trial, a long-term U.S. comparison trial of conventional and organic systems, found that the organic systems use fewer fossil fuels and emit 30 percent less greenhouse gases.[6]

THE REPORT *concluded that our current agricultural production systems are unsustainable and need to change. "'Business as usual' is not an option if we want to achieve environmental sustainability."[3]*

The long-term apple comparison trial conducted by Reganold et al. in Washington State showed that the organic system was more efficient in its energy use, which means emitting fewer greenhouse gases.[7]

The Rodale Institute's organic rotational no-till system can reduce the amount of fossil fuels needed to produce each no-till crop in the rotation by up to 75 percent compared to standard-tilled organic crops.[8]

Energy Used in Different Corn Production Systems

Conventional Tillage:	24.4 gallons per acre (231 liters per hectare)
Conventional No-till:	21 gallons per acre (199 liters per hectare)
Organic Tillage:	12.8 gallons per acre (121 liters per hectare)
Organic No-till:	8.1 gallons per acre (77 liters per hectare)[9]

The best organic systems can have significantly lower energy use than conventional systems, resulting in significantly less greenhouse gas emissions. A peer-reviewed analysis of different production systems found:

Furthermore, the majority of greenhouse gases in farming come from using nitrogen fertilizers, not from farm machinery emissions. Synthetic chemical fertilizers are significant contributors to climate change in terms of the energy used to manufacture them and their contribution to nitrous oxide (N_2O) and methane (CH_4) in the air.

Nitrous oxide is one of the most significant of the greenhouse gases linked to agricultural emissions. One N_2O molecule is equivalent to 310 carbon dioxide (CO_2) molecules in its greenhouse effect in the atmosphere. It has a mean residence time in the atmosphere of 120–150 years and also contributes to the depletion of the ozone layer.

The biggest contributor to human-produced N_2O pollution is the use of synthetic nitrogen fertilizers such as urea and ammonium nitrate in agriculture. Producing these fertilizers contributes additional CO_2 and N_2O to this total.

Synthetic nitrogen fertilizers in farming also add to emissions of CO_2, the compound that accounts for 80 percent of all greenhouse gas emissions. Scientists from the University of Illinois analysed the results of a fifty-year agricultural trial and found that synthetic nitrogen fertilizer resulted in all the carbon residues from the crop disappearing as well as an average loss of around 10,000 kilograms of soil carbon per hectare (8,818 pounds per acre). This is around 36,700 kilograms of carbon dioxide per hectare (32,364 pounds per acre) on top of the many thousands of kilograms of crop residues that are converted into CO_2 every year.[10] The researchers found that the higher the application of synthetic nitrogen fertilizer, the greater the amount of soil carbon lost as CO_2.

On top of emitting fewer greenhouse gases, organic systems sequester CO_2 and store it in the soil as soil organic matter. Consequently organic farms sequester more greenhouse gases than they emit. In a peer-reviewed meta-analysis study using forty-one international comparison trials, Gattinger et al. 2012 reported that organic systems sequestered 2018.5 kilograms of CO_2 per hectare (1780 pounds per acre) per year.[11]

A meta-analysis by Aguilera et al. 2013 of twenty-four comparison trials in Mediterranean climates between organic systems and conventional systems found that the organic systems sequestered 3559.9 kilograms of CO_2 per hectare (3139 pounds per acre) per year. If extrapolated globally, organic systems would sequester an estimated 17.4 gigatons of CO_2.[12]

The Rodale Institute Farming Systems Trial (FST) of organic and conventional cropping systems confirm that organic methods are effective at removing CO_2 from the atmosphere and fixing it as organic matter in the soil.[13]

The FST legume-based organic plots showed sequestration rate of 2,055.2 kilograms of CO_2 per hectare (1,812.4 pounds per acre) per year. Other organic systems produced higher rates of sequestration. The FST manured organic plots showed a sequestration rate of 3,596.6 kilograms of CO_2 per hectare (3,171.7 pounds per acre) per year, and if extrapolated globally would sequester an estimated 17.5 gigatons of CO_2.

Currently CO_2 levels are increasing by 2 ppm per year. 1 ppm CO_2 = 7.76 Gt CO_2. This means we need to remove 15.52 Gt of CO_2 per year from the atmosphere to stabilize CO_2.

The Compost Utilization Trial showed a sequestration rate of 7,340 pounds of CO_2 per acre per year (8,220.8 kilograms of CO_2 per hectare per year) and if extrapolated globally would sequester 40 gigatons of CO_2. This means that the widespread scaling up of organic farming systems can significantly mitigate greenhouse gases and reverse climate change. It can turn agriculture from contributing to climate change to helping avert this potentially catastrophic future for our planet and for humanity.

REGULATORS AND INDUSTRY JUSTIFY PESTICIDE USE

As shown in the previous chapter, regulators generally take the side of the pesticide industry and perpetuate the myth that pesticides are vital for food production.

The main Australian pesticide regulator, the Australian Pesticides and Veterinary Medicines Authority (APVMA), is a good example of a regulator justifying the use of pesticides: "Pesticides and veterinary medicines are vital to quality food and fibre production. Australia's primary production is worth an estimated $30 billion a year with an export value of over $25 billion. Many primary producers rely on pesticides and veterinary medicines to protect their crops and animals from disease and pests."[14]

When pesticides are being reviewed by regulators for adverse effects to human health and the environment, the industry groups always warn that they have no alternative but to use these toxic chemicals as crop protection tools as the justification for not banning them. In the final outcome, it is usually business as usual, or regulators may decide to modify the way pesticides are used to lessen some negative impacts. Rarely are they withdrawn from use to ensure no adverse impacts on human health and the environment.

> **TRILLIONS OF DOLLARS** *have been spent on research into conventional agriculture while at the same time in the last hundred years there has been an almost total neglect of research into organic agriculture.*

Trillions of dollars have been spent on research into conventional agriculture while at the same time in the last hundred years there has been an almost total neglect of research into organic agriculture. A significant proportion of this research funding has been to develop and test the efficacy of synthetic toxic chemicals as pesticides such as herbicides, insecticides, and fungicides.

Some comparison meta-studies, such as the recent ones published in *Nature* and *Agricultural Systems*, suggest that, on average, organic yields are 80 percent of conventional yields.[15] On the other hand, a meta-study by Badgley et al. suggests that the average organic yields are slightly below the chemical intensive yields in the developed world and higher than the conventional average in the developing world.[16] Assuming that the analyses in the journals *Na-*

ture and *Agricultural Systems* are correct, 80 percent is an incredibly small yield gap in relation to the enormous level of research and resources that have been spent to achieve it.

The surprising fact is that millions of organic farmers have worked out how to get reasonable yields without the assistance of scientific research or the regular extension services that conventional agriculture receives.

The main reason for the lower yields in some organic systems has been the fact that research and development into organic systems has been largely ignored. Fifty-two billion dollars is spent annually on agriculture research worldwide. Less than 0.4 percent (four dollars in every thousand) is spent on solutions specific for organic farming systems.[17]

Yet despite this lack of funding, all the data sets from the global meta-comparison studies have examples of organic systems that have the same or higher yields than conventional agriculture.

EXAMPLES OF HIGH-YIELDING ORGANIC SYSTEMS

The following examples of high-yielding organic systems show that under the right conditions organic farming systems can have equal or higher yields than chemical intensive farming systems.

U.S. Agricultural Research Service (ARS) Pecan Trial—The ARS organically managed pecans out-yielded the conventionally managed, chemically fertilized orchard in each of the past five years. Yields at the ARS organic test site surpassed the conventional orchard by eighteen pounds of pecan nuts per tree in 2005 and by twelve pounds per tree in 2007.[18]

The Wisconsin Integrated Cropping Systems Trials—The Wisconsin Integrated Cropping Systems Trials found that organic yields were higher in drought years and the same as conventional in normal weather years. In years with wet weather in the spring the organic yields can suffer when mechanical cultivation of weeds is delayed, and yields were found to be 10 percent lower. This could be corrected by using steam or vinegar for weed control, rather than tillage. The researchers attributed the higher yields in dry years to the organic soil's ability to take in rainfall more quickly. This is due to the higher levels of organic carbon, making the soils more friable and better able to store and capture rain.[19]

Scientific Review by Professor David Pimentel of Cornell University into Twenty-Two-Year-Long Rodale Field Study—The scientific review found:

- The improved soil allowed the organic land to generate yields equal to or greater than the conventional crops after five years.
- The conventional crops collapsed during drought years.
- The organic crops fluctuated only slightly during drought years, due to greater water-holding capacity in the enriched soil.
- The organic crops used 30 percent less fossil energy inputs than the conventional crops.[20]

Rodale Organic Low-/No-Till—The Rodale Institute has been trialing a range of organic low-tillage and no-tillage systems. The 2006 trials resulted in organic yields of 160 bushels an acre (bu/ac) compared to the Berks County average nonorganic corn yield of 130 bu/ac and the regional average of 147 bu/ac.

> The average corn yield of the two organic no-till production fields was 160 bu/ac, while the no-till research field plots averaged 146 bu/ac over 24 plots. The standard-till organic production field yielded 143 bu/ac, while the Farming Systems Trial's (FST's) standard-till organic plots yielded 139 bu/ac in the manure system (which received compost but no vetch N inputs) and 132 bu/ac in the legume system (which received vetch but no compost). At the same time, the FST's non-organic standard-till field yielded 113 bu/ac.[21]

Iowa Trials—The results from the Long Term Agroecological Research (LTAR), a twelve-year collaborative effort between producers and researchers led by Dr. Kathleen Delate of Iowa State University, shows that organic systems can have equal to higher yields than conventional systems. Consistent with several other studies, the data showed that while the organic systems had lower yields in the beginning, by year four they started to exceed the conventional crops. Across all rotations, organic corn harvests averaged

130 bushels per acre while conventional corn yield was 112 bushels per acre. Similarly, organic soybean yield was 45 bushels per acre compared to the conventional yield of 40 bushels per acre in the fourth year. Cost-wise, on average, the organic crops' revenue was twice that of conventional crops due to the savings afforded by not using chemical fertilizers and pesticides and the produce receiving better prices.[22]

MASIPAG Philippines—A research project conducted in the Philippines by MASIPAG found that the yields of organic rice were similar to conventional systems.[23]

Other Examples—Professor George Monbiot, in an article in *The Guardian* in 2000, wrote that for the past 150 years wheat grown with manure has produced consistently higher yields than wheat grown with chemical nutrients in trials in the United Kingdom.[24]

The study into apple production conducted by Washington State University compared the economic and environmental sustainability of conventional, organic, and integrated growing systems in apple production and found similar yields. "Here we report the sustainability of organic, conventional, and integrated apple production systems in Washington State from 1994 to 1999. All three systems gave similar apple yields."[25]

In an article published in the peer-reviewed scientific journal *Nature*, Laurie Drinkwater and colleagues from the Rodale Institute showed that organic farming had better environmental outcomes as well as similar yields of both products and profits when compared to conventional, intensive agriculture.[26]

Dr. Rick Welsh of the Henry A. Wallace Institute reviewed numerous academic publications comparing organic production with conventional production systems in the United States. The data showed that the organic systems were more profitable. This profit was due not always to premiums but to lower production and input costs as well as more consistent yields. Dr. Welsh's study also showed that organic agriculture produced better yields than conventional agriculture in adverse weather events, such as droughts or higher-than-average rainfall.[27]

Nicolas Parrott and Terry Marsden of Cardiff University in the UK authored a report, titled *The Real Green Revolution*, in which they relate case studies that confirm the success of organic and agroecological farming techniques in the developing world. Average cotton yields on farms participating in the organic Maikaal Bio-Cotton Project are 20 percent higher than on neighboring conventional farms in the State of Madhya Pradesh in India. The System of Rice Intensification has increased yields from the usual two to three tons per hectare to yields of six, eight, or ten tons per hectare in Madagascar. The use of bonemeal, rock phosphate, and intercropping with nitrogen-fixing lupin species have significantly contributed to increases in potato yields in Bolivia.[28]

These examples need to be researched to understand why and, importantly, to replicate, improve, and scale up globally. This will close the yield gap and has the potential to overtake the conventional average.

TWO KEY AREAS WHERE ORGANIC HAS HIGH YIELDS

While organic agriculture currently may have lower average yields than the chemically intense industrial agricultural systems in good climate years, there are two areas in which organic agriculture can often have higher yields: under conditions of climate extremes and in traditional smallholder systems. Both of these areas are critical to achieving global food security.

GREATER RESILIENCE IN ADVERSE CONDITIONS

According to research by NASA, the United Nations Framework Convention on Climate Change, and others, the world is seeing increases in the frequency of extreme weather events such as droughts and heavy rainfall. Even if we stopped polluting the planet with greenhouse gases tomorrow, it would take many decades to reverse climate change. Farmers thus have to adapt to the increasing intensity and frequency of adverse and extreme weather events such as droughts and heavy, damaging rainfall.

ORGANIC CORN VS. CONVENTIONAL CORN

The corn grown on the organically managed soil (left) in the long-term Rodale Farming Systems Trial has greater drought tolerance than the conventionally grown corn (right) due to better water-holding capacity.

SOIL CLODS

These jars contain the same soil. The soil on the left has higher levels of organic matter due to long-term organic management compared to the conventionally managed soil on the right. The conventional soil easily erodes and disperses in the water, whereas the organic soil keeps its integrity and resists erosion.

Published studies show that organic farming systems are more resilient to the emerging weather extremes and can produce higher yields than conventional farming systems in such conditions.[29] For instance, the Wisconsin Integrated Cropping Systems Trials found

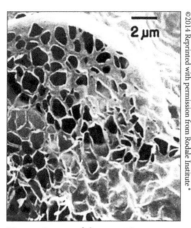

Humus is one of the most important factors of soil organic matter. Its spongelike structure allows it to hold up to thirty times its own weight in water. It is a polymer that glues the soil particles together to give the soil stability, and it holds many of the nutrients that plants need to grow well.

that organic yields were higher in drought years and the same as conventional in normal weather years.[30]

Similarly, the Rodale Farming Systems Trial (FST) showed that the organic systems produced more corn than the conventional system in drought years. The average corn yields during the drought years were from 28 percent to 34 percent higher in the two organic systems. The yields were 6,938 and 7,235 kilograms per hectare in the organic animal and the organic legume systems respectively, compared with 5,333 kilograms per hectare in the conventional system.[31] The researchers attributed the higher yields in the dry years to the ability of the soils on organic farms to better absorb rainfall. This absorption is due to the higher levels of organic carbon in those soils, which makes them more friable and better able to store and capture rainwater, which can then be used for crops.[32]

Research also shows that organic systems use water more efficiently due to better soil structure and higher levels of humus and other organic matter compounds. D. W. Lotter and colleagues collected data over ten years during the Rodale FST. Their research showed that the organic manure system and organic legume system (LEG) treatments improve the soils' water-holding capacity, infiltration rate, and water-capture efficiency. The LEG maize soils averaged a 13 percent higher water content than conventional system soils at the same crop stage, and 7 percent higher than the conventional soils in soybean plots.[33]

The more porous structure of organically treated soil allows rainwater to penetrate more quickly, resulting in less water loss from

FIBL DOK TRIALS: WINTER WHEAT UNDER CONVENTIONAL MANAGEMENT

Andreas Fliessbach, FiBL

Heavy rainfall just after planting in the conventionally managed FiBL DOK trials system causes soil to erode and disperse, preventing much of the water from infiltrating as well as damaging the new crop and lowering yields.

FIBL DOK TRIALS: WINTER WHEAT UNDER ORGANIC MANAGEMENT

Andreas Fliessbach, FiBL

The same soil in the organically managed system of the trials maintains its structure, resists erosion, and allows the heavy rainfall to infiltrate and to be stored in the soil. Consequently there are higher yields when there are heavy rainfall events at planting.

runoff and higher levels of water capture. This was particularly evident during the two days of torrential downpours from Hurricane Floyd in September 1999, when the organic systems captured around double the water of the conventional systems.[34] Long-term scientific trials conducted by the Research Institute of Organic Agriculture (FiBL) in Switzerland comparing organic, biodynamic, and conventional systems (the DOK trials) had similar results, showing that organic systems were more resistant to erosion and better at capturing water.

This information is significant as the majority of world farming systems are rain fed. The world does not have the resources to irrigate all of the agricultural lands, nor should such a project be started such as damming the world's watercourses, pumping from all the underground aquifers, and building millions of kilometers of channels because this would cause an unprecedented environmental disaster.

Improving the efficiency of rain-fed agricultural systems through organic practices is the most efficient, cost-effective, environmentally sustainable, and practical solution to ensure reliable food production in the increasing weather extremes being caused by climate change.

THE REPORT NOTES *that despite the introduction of conventional agriculture in Africa, food production per person is 10 percent lower now than in the 1960s.*

SMALLHOLDER FARMER YIELDS

The other critical area where research is showing higher yields for good practice organic systems is in traditional smallholder systems. This is very important information as over 85 percent of the world's farmers fall into this category.

A 2008 report by the United Nations Conference on Trade and Development (UNCTAD) and the United Nations Environment Programme (UNEP) that assessed 114 projects in 24 African countries covering 2 million hectares and 1.9 million farmers found that organic agriculture increases yields in sub-Saharan Africa by 116 percent. There was a 128 percent increase for East Africa. The report notes that despite the introduction of conventional agriculture in Africa, food production per person is 10 percent lower now than in the 1960s. "The evidence presented in this study supports the argument that organic agriculture can be more conducive to food security in Africa than most conventional production systems, and that it is more likely to be sustainable in the long term," stated Supachai Panitchpakdi, secretary general of UNCTAD, and Achim Steiner, executive director of UNEP.[35]

Badgley et al. from the University of Michigan compared a global dataset of 293 examples of organic versus conventional food production and estimated the average yield ratio. The comparison was divided into different food categories for the developed and the developing world. The researchers found that for most food categories, the average organic yield ratio was slightly less than the average in the developed world and greater than the average in the developing world. Most significantly, the study showed that organic farming can yield up to three times more food on individual farms in developing countries, as compared to conventional farms.[36]

This information is especially relevant as Food and Agriculture Organization of the United Nations (FAO) data shows that 80 percent of the food in the developing world comes from smallholder farmers.[37] The developing world is also the region where most of the 850 million hungry people in the world live, the majority of which are smallholder farmers. With a more than 100 percent increase in food production in these traditional farming systems, organic agriculture provides an ideal solution to end hunger and ensure global food security.

Information published by the ETC Group shows that 70 percent of the world's food is produced by smallholders and only 30 percent by the agribusiness sector.[38] Increasing the yields in the 30 percent of food that comes from the agribusiness sector will show little benefit for two reasons.

Firstly, this sector is already high yielding, and it has very little scope for large increases in yields, such as the more than 100 percent that can be achieved by organic methods in traditional smallholder systems. Secondly, this sector is largely focused on the commodity supply chain. The large food surpluses produced in this sector have not lowered the number of people who are hungry, despite the fact that the world currently produces more than double the amount of food needed to feed everyone. According to FAO figures, the number of hungry has been steadily increasing since 1995. Simply put: the people who need this food the most cannot afford to buy it. On the other hand the people who need it the least are consuming too much, leading to an obesity epidemic around the world. Increasing the production in the agribusiness sector will not solve the current hunger problem, as it cannot do it now, and will most likely increase the obesity epidemic.

INCREASING THE YIELDS IN SMALLHOLDER FARMERS IS THE KEY TO FOOD SECURITY

About 50 percent of the world's hungry are smallholder farmers and 20 percent are the landless poor who rely on smallholders for their employment.[39]

Logically, increasing the yields in the smallholder farmer sector is the key to ending hunger and achieving food security. Organic methods are the most suitable because the necessary methods and inputs can be sourced on farm as well as locally at very little to no cost to the farmers. Conventional systems have largely failed to provide consistently higher yields to the poorest farmers because the expensive synthetic chemical inputs have to be purchased. Most of these farmers do not have the income to do this. It is an inappropriate economic model for the world's most vulnerable farmers, whereas organic agriculture is an appropriate model.

An example of sustainable farming's relevance to smallholder farmers is found in research conducted in the Philippines by MASIPAG. The yields of organic rice were similar to conventional systems; however, a comparison of the income between similar-sized conventional and organic farms found that the average income for organic farms was 23,599 pesos compared to 15,643 pesos for the conventional farms. Very significantly, when the household living expenses were deducted from the income, the study found that the organic farms had a surplus of 5,967 pesos whereas the conven-

AVERAGE MEAN GRAIN YIELDS FOR FOUR CEREALS AND ONE PULSE CROP FROM TIGRAY, NORTHERN ETHIOPIA, 2000-2006 INCLUSIVE

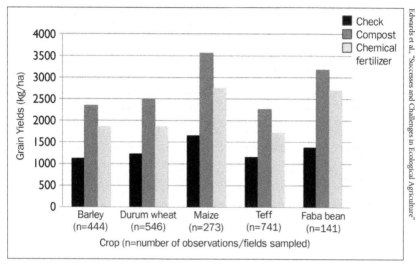

In every case the yield from applying compost was more than 100 percent higher than the traditional systems (Check) and was higher than using chemical fertilizers.

tional farms had a loss of 4,546 pesos at the end of the year, driving them further into debt.[40]

TIGRAY, ETHIOPIA

Another good example is the Tigray Project, managed by the Institute of Sustainable Development (ISD) in Tigray, Ethiopia. This was an area regularly affected by famines that caused many people to die. ISD worked in cooperation with the farmers to revegetate their landscape to restore the local ecology and hydrology. The biomass from this vegetation was then sustainably harvested to make compost and to feed biogas digesters. This compost was applied to the crop fields. The result after a few years was more than 100 percent increases in yields, better water use efficiency, and greater pest and disease resistance in the crops.

The farmers used the seeds of their own landraces, which had been developed over millennia to be locally adapted to the climate, soils, and the major pests and diseases. The best of these farmer-bred varieties proved very responsive to producing high yields under organic conditions.

The major advantage of this system was that the seeds and the compost were sourced locally at little or no cost to the farmers, whereas the seeds and synthetic chemical inputs in the conventional systems had to be purchased. Not only did the organic system have higher yields, it produced a much better net return to the farmers.[41]

According to Dr. Sue Edwards, the lead author of the Tigray Project, the farmers who used compost earned U.S. $2,925 per hectare compared to U.S. $1,725 per hectare earned by farmers using chemical fertilizers.[42]

This project, using simple, appropriate organic methods, took a region that was previously regularly affected by severe famines harsh enough to kill people, through to a food surplus and relative prosperity. The people could now afford to eat well, to buy clothes, send their children to school, pay for medical treatment, afford transport into town, and build adequate houses.

The Tigray Project started in 1996 in four local communities in the central, eastern, and southern parts of the Tigray Regional State and was implemented by the Institute for Sustainable Development (ISD). Third World Network (TWN) provided the initial funding. This project is still ongoing with ISD working with the Ethiopian Bureau of Agriculture and Rural Development, *woreda* (district) experts, and development agents to continue executing the Tigray Project. The funding from several donor agencies is assisting in scaling up the project's scope so that more regions in Ethiopia can adopt the practices.[43]

At the time of writing much of east and southern Africa, including Ethiopia, are in the midst of the worst drought in 60 years with tens of millions of people in need of food aid due to crop failure. The farmers in Tigray province who are part of the ISD project are not affected. Their crop yields are stable due to the better water capture and storage in soils that are treated with compost and have reasonable levels of soil organic matter. [44]

HEALTH PER ACRE

One of the best examples of measuring nutrition in agriculture comes from a book written by Dr. Vandana Shiva and Dr. Vaibhav Singh, titled *Health Per Acre*. This book compared the nutrition produced per acre in a typical high-biodiversity organic farm (multiple food crops) in India against the nutrition produced by a typical conventional farm that grows only a few commodity crops. A valid comparison between the two systems had never been done before. Most studies compare the yield of organic systems with the yield of the conventional system per acre, per crop, whereas in reality the two production systems are very different. Most organic farms, especially in developing countries, are mixed systems with multiple crops of food, such as numerous vegetables, fruits, grains, pulses, as well as animal products like eggs, milk, and meat. On the other hand, most conventional systems tend to just produce a few or a single crop, primarily cash crops destined for commodity trading markets.

The research project reported in *Health Per Acre* found that when all the nutrients in the crops were analyzed, rather than the standard measurement of pounds of gross produce per acre (kilos per hectare), the diverse organic system produced significantly more vitamins, minerals, and other key nutrients needed for a healthy diet than the conventional system.

Measuring total nutrition from a farming system is a very important and critical methodology to determine food security and nutrition. The current system is just based on measuring only the calories, most of which are empty of real nutrition—the vitamins, minerals, and other nutrients needed for good health.

Over 850 million people are classified as food insecure, meaning there are periods of the year when they do not have any food to eat. There are more than one billion extra people in the world who get enough calories but are deficient in key nutrients. For instance, most women in rural India, hundreds of millions, suffer from anemia due to iron deficiencies in their diet. This leads to a whole suite of health and reproductive problems. Iron deficiencies in rural women can easily be corrected by growing a few green leafy vegetables and including them in a daily diet. It is the same with beta-carotene deficiencies. Growing leafy and yellow fruits and vegetables can easily correct these problems.

The research discussed in *Health Per Acre* showed that converting all of India's farms into biodiverse regenerative organic farms would not only correct all these deficiencies, it would yield enough nutrition to supply two Indias with a diverse diet of healthy nutritious food.[45]

RESEARCH SHOWS *that organic pesticides are used in amounts over 90 percent smaller than the synthetic pesticides used in conventional farming.*

————————✂————————

REDUCING THE RISK FROM SYNTHETIC PESTICIDES BY REPLACING THEM

One of the most effective ways to reduce the health and environmental risks from pesticides is to replace them with non-chemical methods.

There is a lot of misinformation out there about the use of pesticides in organic farming. Several articles have stated that the natural pesticides used in organic farming are just as toxic as the synthetic chemical pesticides used in conventional farming. These articles further state that the majority of pesticides that people consume are the protective compounds produced by plants to protect themselves from pests and diseases, not synthetic pesticides. This misinformation needs to be corrected.

Organic farming considerably reduces the need for pesticides by using cultural and ecological management systems as the primary control for pests, weeds, and diseases, with a limited use of natural biocides of mineral, plant, and biological origin as the tools of last resort.

The pesticides used in organic systems are from natural sources and are permitted to be used only if they rapidly biodegrade or are nontoxic, which means that there are no residues on the products that people consume or that residues are natural compounds that people regularly consume with no ill effects. By using cultural and ecological methods as the primary management tools with the aims of firstly preventing pests and secondly controlling them, the use of these pesticides is minimal. Unlike conventional farming, in which pesticides are liberally used as the primary method to control pests, diseases and weeds; organic pesticides are used as the tools of last resort. Research shows that organic pesticides are used in amounts over 90 percent smaller than the synthetic pesticides used in conventional farming.[46]

If there are any residues, they are non-toxic, however very significantly, because unlike most synthetic pesticides that are systemic and absorbed inside the food, organic pesticides are non-systemic, meaning that they can be easily washed off food.

NONTOXIC SPRAYS

Many of the compounds used to control pests and diseases in organic agriculture, such as vegetable oils, soap, and clay, are nontoxic. Some of these nontoxic compounds may leave small residues on food. The consumption of a minute amount of clay or vegetable oil is not going to cause any problems. If there are any minute residues of vegetable oil on organic food, it would be significantly less than the amount of oil in a salad dressing or in cooked food. Like with natural soap, regular exposure to small amounts is usually regarded as a good thing for most people. Any residues of soap on food would be significantly less than the amount of soap people would absorb through their skin when washing their hands or taking a normal shower or bath.

NATURAL MINERALS

Natural mineral compounds like copper sulfate or sulfur may leave small residues. These are used as natural fungicides or insecticides. Unlike synthetic fungicides, both copper and sulfur are essential nutrients for humans. In fact, most multivitamin formulations include copper sulfate to correct nutrient deficiencies. In most places in the world, these minerals are also essential plant nutrients as many soils are deficient in them, apart from a few areas where they have been overused.

BOTANICAL SPRAYS

There are some toxic organic pesticides, such as natural pyrethrums. While their short-term toxicity, the LD_{50}, is as toxic as many synthetic pesticides, they rapidly biodegrade and are usually completely degraded by ultraviolet light within twenty-four hours of being used. These compounds are quickly degraded by the body temperature of mammals. They are highly toxic to cold-blooded animals, such as insects, but they have no long-term toxicity for mammals. Short-term toxicity is the primary concern with these sprays, as the people applying these pesticides can be exposed to significant amounts if they are not wearing appropriate protective equipment and clothing. However, for consumers there should be no residues. To the best of my knowledge, I have never seen any survey of pesticide residues that have found these compounds on food.

BIOLOGICAL PESTICIDES

There are several biological pesticides that can be used in organic farming. The advantage of their use is that they only kill the target pest and do not harm non-target species, such as beneficial insects, birds, wildlife, and people. One of the most common of these pesticides is *Bacillus thuringiensis* (Bt). Bt puts out toxic compounds that cause inflammation and tissue damage in the organs of specific insect pests such as caterpillars.

The genes from Bt have been inserted into several genetically modified crops so that the plants produce pesticides themselves. The GM industry argues that this is no different from what organic farmers do when they spray Bt bacteria, but this is a massive distortion of facts. Organic farmers spray live bacteria onto the crop, not the Bt toxins. During the night and in the early morning, pests eat the bacteria, infecting them so that the bacteria release their toxins and eventually kill the pests. Bt are killed by ultraviolet light, so usually none will survive more than a day or two, so consumers will not be affected by the toxins produced by Bt.

On the other hand, every cell of a Bt GMO plant and its produce contain the Bt toxin, so livestock and people are consuming these pesticide compounds.

See chapter 1 for a more thorough discussion of this issue.

As stated previously, if there are any residues from any of the plant protection compounds used in organic agriculture, not only are they non-toxic, but they can be easily washed off.

PLANT PROTECTIVE COMPOUNDS

Some media spin doctors claim that the protective compounds in plants are the primary sources of pesticides people consume, and not synthetic pesticides, but this is simply not the case. Many plants put out compounds to protect themselves from pests and diseases. The majority of these protective compounds are antioxidants, such as lycopene in tomatoes, resveratrol in grapes and red wine, and anthocyanins in blueberries and other fruits. When people consume these antioxidants, they get the protective benefits as well.

Some plants do emit highly toxic pesticides like natural pyrethrums, but we tend not to consume these toxic plants as food. Justifying the addition of toxic synthetic pesticides to food by arguing that we are already exposed to pesticides in food is not only illogical, it is very dangerous. Given the possible adverse synergistic effects that can occur, adding more pesticides to our food could create a toxic cocktail of chemicals. We would be smart to avoid even the smallest synthetic pesticide residues when we do not have any scientific evidence to show that they are safe.

ECO—FUNCTIONAL INTENSIFICATION

An emerging strategy for replacing pesticides, including natural ones, advocates using ecological management systems that can provide functional services, such as using natural enemies to control pests. The key is to identify these eco-functions and then intensify them in the farming systems so that they replace the need for insecticides. Eco-functional intensification (EFI) is used in organic agriculture to utilize ecological processes rather than chemical intensification. A good example of this is adding insectaries into the farming system. Insectaries are groups of plants that attract and host the beneficial arthropods (insects, bugs, spiders, etc.) and higher animal species. These are the species that eat arthropod pests in farms, orchards, and gardens. They are known collectively as beneficials or natural enemies.

Many beneficial arthropods have a range of host plants. Some useful species—such as parasitic wasps, hoverflies, and lacewings—have carnivorous larvae that eat pests; however, the adult stages need nectar and pollen from flowers to become sexually mature and reproduce. Flowers provide beneficial arthropods with concentrated forms of food (pollen and nectar) and increase their chances of surviving, immigrating, and staying in the area. Very importantly, flowers provide mating sites for beneficials, allowing them to increase in numbers. Without these flowers on a farm the beneficial species die and do not reproduce. Most farming systems eliminate these types of plants as weeds, so consequently they do not have enough beneficials to get effective pest control.

The current loss of biodiversity on this planet is causing the greatest extinction event since the end of the Cretaceous period. Agriculture is one of the main causes due to both habitat loss by clearing forests and the disruption caused by synthetic chemicals. Organic agriculture has a role in conserving and, equally important, increasing and utilizing biodiversity through the concept of eco-functional intensification.

THE PUSH–PULL SYSTEM

Pull: The Napier grass attracts the moths to lay their eggs in it instead of the maize (corn). Push: The desmodium repels the moths. Desmodium suppresses weeds, especially striga.

Desmodium suppresses weeds, adds nitrogen (so there is no need for synthetic nitrogen fertilizers), conserves the soil, repels pests, and provides high-protein stock feed.

The Napier grass is progressively cut and fed to a cow. The excess fresh milk is sold daily as a cash income.

EFI is about utilizing the science of applied agroecology to actively increase the biodiversity in agricultural systems to reduce pests rather than using the conventional approach, based on reductionist monocultures that rely on externally sourced toxic synthetic inputs.

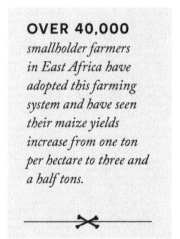

OVER 40,000 *smallholder farmers in East Africa have adopted this farming system and have seen their maize yields increase from one ton per hectare to three and a half tons.*

Considering the small average yield difference between chemically intensive and organic farming systems, the more than $50 billion spent annually on conventional farming would be better spent on researching non-chemical, science-based ecological solutions.

PUSH-PULL SYSTEM

The push-pull method in maize (corn) is an excellent example of a science-based eco-functional intensification system that integrates several ecological elements to achieve substantial increases in yields. The possibilities of this method are significant because maize is the key food staple for smallholder farmers in Africa, Latin America, and in many parts of Asia.

Corn stem borers are one of the most significant pests in maize. Conventional agriculture relies on a number of toxic, synthetic pesticides to control these pests. Recently it has started to adopt genetically engineered varieties of corn that produce their own pesticides to combat this pest.

The push-pull system was developed by scientists in Kenya at the International Centre of Insect Physiology and Ecology (ICIPE); Rothamsted Research, UK; and with the collaboration of other partners.

Silverleaf desmodium is planted in the crop to repel stem borers and to attract the natural enemies of the pest. The desmodium gives off phenolic compounds that repel the stem borer moth. Its root exudates also stop the growth of many weed species, including striga, which is a serious parasitic weed of maize. Napier grass, a host plant of the moth, is planted outside the field as a trap crop for the stem borer. The desmodium repels (pushes) the pests from the maize and the Napier grass attracts (pulls) the stem borers out of the field to lay their eggs on it in instead of the maize. The sharp silica hairs and sticky exudates on the Napier grass also kill the stem borer larvae when they hatch, breaking the life cycle and reducing pest numbers.

Over 40,000 smallholder farmers in East Africa have adopted this farming system and have seen their maize yields increase from one ton per hectare to three and a half tons. This is a more than 300 percent increase in yields and shows the huge benefits of shifting research away from toxic chemicals to science-based ecological systems.

High yields are not the only benefits. The system does not need synthetic nitrogen because desmodium is a legume and fixes nitrogen. Soil erosion is prevented due to a permanent ground cover. Very significantly, the system also provides quality fodder for stock.

One farming innovation to improve this system has been to systematically strip harvest the Napier grass to use as fresh fodder for livestock. Livestock can also graze down the field after the maize is harvested. Many push-pull farmers integrate a dairy cow into the system and sell the milk that is surplus to their family needs to provide a regular source of income. This method has provided the farm families with food and income security and has taken them from hunger and desperate poverty into relative prosperity.

African farmers have adapted push-pull to numerous other crops such as tomatoes, chili, sorghum, teff, millet, and mangoes.

There are many examples of other innovative EFI systems that are being developed, such as the system of rice intensification, organic no-/low-till systems (i.e., cover cropping and pasture cropping), agroforestry, and holistic grazing.

THE URGENT NEED FOR MORE RESEARCH

Research into organic agriculture has been chronically underfunded. Trillions of dollars have gone into conventional and GMO research; the organic sector receives a tiny fraction of this. This situation needs to be rectified so that the need for toxic synthetic pesticides is significantly reduced.

Africa fortunately sees the multiple benefits of organic systems, with the African Union Commission adopting Ecological Organic Agriculture as part of the mix of solutions needed to achieve food security.

Given the small yield difference that has been achieved with trillions of dollars and countless thousands of researchers compared to what organic farmers have achieved when left largely to their own devices, it would have to be argued that the substantial proportion of the funding into conventional agriculture has been a very poor use of valuable research funds. Also given that the new research into organic systems is starting to show very impressive increases in yields, it is logical to argue that research into organic agriculture is a far better use of these research funds.

NOTES

[1] United Nations Millennium Ecosystem Assessment Synthesis Report, March 2005.

[2] David Tilman, F. Fargione, B. Wolff, C. D'Antonio, A. Dobson, R. Howarth, D. Schindler, W. Schlesinger, D. Simberloff, and D. Swackhamer, "Forecasting Agriculturally Driven Global Environmental Change," *Science* 292 (April 13, 2001): 281–84.

[3] Ian Scoones, "The Politics of Global Assessments: The Case of the International Assessment of Agricultural Knowledge, Science and Technology for Development (IAASTD)," *Journal of Peasant Studies* 36, no. 3 (2009): 547–571; United Nations Millennium Ecosystem Assessment Synthesis Report, March 2005; Tilman et al., "Forecasting Agriculturally Driven Global Environmental Change."

[4] D. G. Hole, A. J. Perkins, J. D. Wilson, I. H. Alexander, P. V. Grice, A. D. Evans, "Does Organic Farming Benefit Biodiversity?," *Biological Conservation* 122 (2005): 113–30.

[5] Grain, (2013), Commentary IV: Food, Climate Change and Healthy Soils: The Forgotten Link, in UNCTAD Trade and Environment Review 2013, Wake Up Before it is too Late, Ed. Ulrich Hoffman, UNCTAD/DITC/TED/2012/3, United Nations Publication ISSN 1810-5432.

[6] David Pimentel, Paul Hepperly, James Hanson, David Douds, and Rita Seidel, "Environmental, Energetic and Economic Comparisons of Organic and Conventional Farming Systems," *Bioscience* 55, no. 7 (July 2005): 573–82.

[7] John P. Reganold, Jerry D. Glover, Preston K. Andrews, and Herbert R. Hinman, "Sustainability of Three Apple Production Systems," *Nature* 410 (March 15, 2001): 926–930.

[8] Timothy LaSalle and Paul Hepperly, "Regenerative Organic Farming: A Solution to Global Warming," Rodale Institute, 2008.

[9] Pimentel et al., "Environmental, Energetic and Economic Comparisons."

[10] S. A. Khan, R. L. Mulvaney, T. R. Ellsworth, and C. W. Boast, "The Myth of Nitrogen Fertilization for Soil Carbon Sequestration," *Journal of Environmental Quality* 36, no. 6 (October 24, 2007): 1821–32; R. L. Mulvaney, S. A. Khan, and T. R. Ellsworth, "Synthetic Nitrogen Fertilizers Deplete Soil Nitrogen: A Global Dilemma for Sustainable Cereal Production," *Journal of Environmental Quality* 38 (2009): 2295–2314.

[11] Andreas Gattinger, Adrian Muller, Matthias Haenia, Colin Skinner, Andreas Fliessbach, Nina Buchman, Paul Mäder, Matthias Stolze, Pete Smith, Nadia El-Hage Scialabba, and Urs Niggli, "Enhanced Top Soil Carbon Stocks under Organic Farming, *PNAS* 109, no. 44 (October 30, 2012): 18231.

[12] Eduardo Aguilera, Luis Lassaletta, Andreas Gattinger, Benjamín S. Gimeno, "Managing Soil Carbon for Climate Change Mitigation and Adaptation in Mediterranean Cropping Systems: A Meta-Analysis," *Agriculture, Ecosystems and Environment* 168 (2013): 25–36.

[13] LaSalle and Hepperly, "Regenerative Organic Farming"; *The Farming Systems Trial: Celebrating 30 Years*, Rodale Institute, http://rodaleinstitute.org/our-work/farming-systems-trial/farming-systems-trial-30-year-report/ (accessed October 22, 2013).

[14] APVMA, "About the APVMA: Factsheet."

[15] Verena Seufert, Navin Ramankutty, and Jonathan A. Foley, "Comparing the Yields of Organic and Conventional Agriculture," *Nature* 485 (May 2012): 229–32, http://www.nature.com/nature/journal/v485/n7397/full/nature11069.html; Tomek de Ponti, Bert Rijk, and Martin van Ittersum, "The Crop Yield Gap between Organic and Conventional Agriculture," *Agricultural Systems* 108 (2012): 1–9.

[16] Catherine Badgley et al., "Organic Agriculture and the Global Food Supply," *Renewable Agriculture and Food Systems* 22, no. 2 (2007): 86–108.

[17] Urs Niggli, "Sustainability of Organic Food Production: Challenges and Innovations," *Proceedings of the Nutrition Society*, forthcoming.

[18] Alfredo Flores, "Organic Pecans: Another Option for Growers," *Agricultural Research* magazine, U.S. Agricultural Research Service, November/December 2008, http://www.ars.usda.gov/is/AR/archive/nov08/pecans1108.pdf.

[19] Jean-Paul Chavas, Joshua L. Posner, and Janet L. Hedtcke, "Organic and Conventional Production Systems in the Wisconsin Integrated Cropping Systems Trial: II. Economic and Risk Analysis 1993–2006," *Agronomy Journal* 101, no. 2 (2009): 253–60, http://wicst.wisc.edu/wp-content/uploads/pages-from-wicst-econ-aj2009.pdf.

[20]   David Pimentel et al., "Environmental, Energetic and Economic Comparisons of Organic and Conventional Farming Systems," *Bioscience* 55, no. 7 (July 2005): 573–82, http://www.ce.cmu.edu/~gdrg/readings/2007/02/20/Pimental_EnvironmentalEnergeticAndEconomic ComparisonsOfOrganicAndConventionalFarmingSystems.pdf.

[21]   Rodale Institute, "Organic No-Till," http://www.rodaleinstitute.org/no-till_ revolution (accessed January 2014).

[22]   Bob Turnbull, "Research Shows Organic Corn, Soybean Yields Can Exceed Conventional," *Organic & Non-GMO Report*, January 2010, http://www. non-gmoreport.com/articles/feb10/organic_corn_soybean_yields_exceed _conventional.php.

[23]   Lorenz Bachman, Elizabeth Cruzada, and Sarah Wright, "Food Security and Farmer Empowerment: A Study of the Impacts of Farmer-Led Sustainable Agriculture in the Philippines," MASIPAG, Anos Los Banos, Laguna 4000, Philippines, 2009.

[24]   George Monbiot, "Organic Farming Will Feed the World," *The Guardian*, August 24, 2000.

[25]   John P. Reganold et al., "Sustainability of Three Apple Production Systems," *Nature* 410 (April 2001): 926–30.

[26]   Laurie E. Drinkwater, Peggy Wagoner, and Marianne Sarrantonio, "Legume-Based Cropping Systems Have Reduced Carbon and Nitrogen Losses," *Nature* 396 (November 1998): 262–65, http://www.nature.com/nature/journal/v396/n6708/abs/396262a0. html.

[27]   Rick Welsh, "The Economics of Organic Grain and Soybean Production in the Midwestern United States," Policy Studies Report No. 13, Henry A. Wallace Institute for Sustainable Agriculture, May 1999.

[28]   Nicholas Parrott and Terry Marsden, *The Real Green Revolution: Organic and Agroecological Farming in the South* (Canonbury Villas, London: Greenpeace Environmental Trust, 2002).

[29]   Pimentel et al., "Environmental, Energetic and Economic Comparisons of Organic and Conventional Farming Systems"; Drinkwater, Wagoner, and Sarrantonio, "Legume-Based Cropping Systems Have Reduced Carbon and Nitrogen Losses"; Welsh, "The Economics of Organic Grain and Soybean Production."

[30]   Chavas, Posner, and Hedtcke, "Organic and Conventional Production Systems in the Wisconsin Integrated Cropping Systems."

[31]   Pimentel et al., "Environmental, Energetic and Economic Comparisons of Organic and Conventional Farming Systems."

[32]   LaSalle and Hepperly, "Regenerative Organic Farming."

[33]   D. W. Lotter, R. Seidel, and W. Liebhart, "The Performance of Organic and Conventional Cropping Systems in an Extreme Climate Year," *American Journal of*

Alternative Agriculture 18, no. 3 (2003): 146–54, http://www.donlotter.net/lotter_ajaa_article.pdf.

[34] Ibid.

[35] Rachel Hine and Jules Pretty, *Organic Agriculture and Food Security in Africa*, United Nations Environment Programme, United Nations Conference on Trade and Development, September 2008, http://www.unctad.org/en/docs/ditcted200715_en.pdf.

[36] Badgley et al., "Organic Agriculture and the Global Food Supply."

[37] Food and Agriculture Organization of the United Nations, "The Challenge," chapter 1 in *Save and Grow*, Rome, 2011, http://www.fao.org/ag/save-and-grow/en/1/index.html.

[38] ETC Group, "Who Will Feed Us? Questions for the Food and Climate Crises," November 1, 2009, http://www.etcgroup.org/content/who-will-feed-us.

[39] Ibid.

[40] Bachman, Cruzada, and Wright, "Food Security and Farmer Empowerment."

[41] Sue Edwards, Tewolde Berhan Gebre Egziabher, and Hailu Araya, "Successes and Challenges in Ecological Agriculture: In Experiences from Tigray, Ethiopia," in *Climate Change and Food Systems Resilience in Sub-Saharan Africa*, ed. Lim Li Ching, Sue Edwards, and Nadia El-Hage Scialabba (Rome: Food and Agriculture Organization of the United Nations, 2011), 231–94. Available online at www.fao.org/docrep/014/i2230e/i2230e09.pdf.

[42] Dr. Sue Edwards, personal communication.

[43] Ibid.

[44] http://www.fao.org/emergencies/emergency-types/drought/en/. Dr Sue Edwards Pers. Com.

[45] Dr. Vandana Shiva and Dr. Vaibhav Singh, *Health Per Acre* (Navdanya, India: 2011).

[46] Paul Maeder et al., "Soil Fertility and Biodiversity in Organic Farming," Science 296 (May 2002): 1694–97, http://www.sciencemag.org/content/296/5573/1694.short.

PROTECTING
our Children
and our Future

The most important issues documented throughout this book are the special needs of the unborn and growing children. This group is the most vulnerable to the harm caused by chemicals. The research shows that they are being exposed to cocktails of chemicals even before they are born. Young children have the highest levels of pesticide exposure due to their food consumption in relation to their body weight. Of particular concern is that the fetus and newborn possess lower concentrations of protective serum proteins than adults. A major consequence of this vulnerability is a greater susceptibility to cancers and developmental neurotoxicity, where the poison damages the developing nervous system. The unborn and young children are also vulnerable to chemicals that cause epimutations, which will affect how their genes influence their development as they grow to adulthood.

They are more vulnerable than adults to the effects of endocrine disrupters because their tissues and organs are still developing and rely on balanced hormone signals to ensure that they develop in orderly sequences. Small disruptions in these hormone signals by endocrine-disrupting chemicals can significantly alter the way these body parts and metabolic systems develop. These altered effects will not only last a lifetime; they can be passed on to future generations.

A large body of published, peer-reviewed scientific research shows that pesticide exposure in unborn and growing children is linked to:

- Cancers as children and as adults
- Thyroid disorders
- Immune system problems
- Lower IQs
- Attention deficit hyperactivity disorder (ADHD)
- Autism spectrum disorders
- Lack of physical coordination
- Loss of temper—anger management issues
- Bipolar/schizophrenia spectrum of illnesses
- Depression
- Digestive system problems
- Cardiovascular disease
- Reproductive problems (as adults)
- Deformities of the genital-urinary systems
- Changes to metabolic systems, including childhood obesity and diabetes

The current pesticide-testing methodologies use adolescent and adult animals. Consequently, they will not detect adverse health issues that are specific to the unborn and children. The U.S. EPA's approach of lowering residues by a factor of ten for children is based on data-free assumptions, especially since the evidence coming from endocrine disruption and non-monotonic doses shows that in many cases there is no threshold, which means that there is no safe level of exposure.

THE USE OF PEER-REVIEWED SCIENTIFIC STUDIES PUBLISHED IN CREDIBLE JOURNALS

There is a critical need for all regulatory decisions to be made on the basis of credible scientific evidence, largely based on peer-reviewed studies published in credible journals. The interpretation of scientific data is not always clear-cut because of many variables, especially where there are gaps in the data. Publishing studies in journals so that they are available for all the relevant stakeholders to read and analyze allows for a wider and more critical debate over the data and encourages a more rigorous process in reaching conclusions.

The use of unpublished, commercial-in-confidence industry studies, hidden from independent scientists, researchers, and the public, must be stopped. These studies are the results of egregious conflicts of interest as well as a non-transparent process. As parents, we have the right to know what studies are being used to make regulatory decisions about poisonous residues in our food, and we have every right to be suspicious and doubtful of any decision-making process in which regulators and the industry are deliberately hiding the facts from us. What are they trying to hide, and why are they hiding it?

One of the most important aspects of this scientific process is that studies should clearly document the materials and methods used in research experiments. Many studies showing the adverse effects of pesticides and problems with current regulatory methodologies are criticized through academic and political debates. The accepted way to resolve the credibility of research is to accurately repeat the experiment by using the material and methods described in the published paper to see if they consistently produce the same results. This will in most cases confirm whether or not the research conclusions are correct.

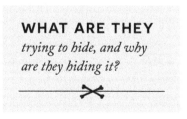

WHAT ARE THEY
trying to hide, and why are they hiding it?

One of the methods used at times by the pesticide industry and regulators to rebut and discredit studies that find adverse health outcomes is to state that industry studies fail to report the same adverse outcomes. This book has given numerous examples of studies showing adverse health effects caused by pesticides. Studies that do not find adverse outcomes do not negate studies that find adverse outcomes. It is unscientific nonsense to say just because some studies do not find evidence of cancer, developmental neurotoxicity, endocrine disruption, and other diseases that these studies invalidate the studies that find these outcomes. All it means is that under different criteria there can be different outcomes.

The industry studies used to refute studies that find adverse outcomes are largely unpublished and are usually based on different criteria than the peer-reviewed studies they are meant to refute. Setting up research using different criteria will most likely result in different outcomes. When the outcomes of these "similar" studies do not confirm the results of the study with adverse health outcomes, the pesticide industry and regulators use them to discredit the potentially profit-damaging study and dismiss its results.

A good analogy would be if an organization performed a few studies on a select number of elderly people who smoke tobacco and then announced that "studies" show no evidence that smoking reduces a person's life span, as these people have lived long lives while smoking every day. Tobacco proponents could then use these biased studies as "evidence" that the hundreds of other studies linking smoking tobacco to numerous health issues should be ignored because the results are "not proven." Big Tobacco did this for decades. They would present studies showing that tobacco did not cause the various illnesses attributed to it, saying that the studies that found these illnesses must be wrong, poor quality, an inadequate methodology, or some other excuse to discredit them.

Dan Fagin, in a comment article that he wrote in *Nature* in 2012, a few months after publication of the comprehensive meta-review on endocrine disruption by Vandenberg et al., gave the following example. He mentions two separate studies that were conducted on the plasticizer bisphenol A (BPA) to assess if it is an endocrine disrupter. One study was conducted by the U.S. Food and Drug Administration (FDA) and the other by a private firm that was contracted by industry. Neither study found evidence of endocrine disruption by BPA, despite numerous other studies finding this.[1] Vandenberg et al., for example, reported that "In 2006, vom Saal and Welshons . . . examined the low-dose BPA literature, identifying more than 100 studies published as of July 2005 that reported significant effects of BPA below the established LOAEL [lowest observable adverse effect level], of which 40 studies reported adverse effects below the 50μg/kg·d safe dose set by the EPA and U.S. Food and Drug Administration (FDA)."[2]

Substantially more studies have been published since 2005 showing the endocrine-disrupting effects of BPA. Because regulatory authorities take a reactionary approach rather than a precautionary approach, one study confirming the status quo tends to take precedence over the many studies that challenge it.

According to Fagin, largely because of these two studies, neither the U.S. FDA nor the U.S. EPA will alter their risk assessments for BPA despite more than a hundred published, peer-reviewed scientific studies showing adverse health effects. "The FDA still says that BPA has no adverse effects at levels below 50 milligrams per kilogram of body weight per day—a level that vom Saal contends should actually be two million times lower, at 25 nanograms."[3]

The vom Saal quoted by Fagin is Dr. Frederick vom Saal, PhD, a neurobiologist and professor at the University of Missouri—Columbia. He is a leading and pioneering scientist in the field of endocrine disrupters and has been since the 1970s. He was one of the coauthors of the Vandenberg et al. meta-review. Vom Saal stated that both of the studies conducted by the industry and the FDA used criteria that were not suitable for finding the effects of endocrine disruption. Parts of the design of the two experiments were regarded by vom Saal and other expert researchers in the field of endocrine disruption as insensitive to low-dose effects, and consequently they would not be found in the results.

Vandenberg et al. give many examples of the way the differences in the design of experiments will result in outcomes that will not confirm the earlier studies. "In fact, the NTP [National Toxicology Program] low-dose panel itself suggested that factors such as strain differences, diet, caging and housing conditions, and seasonal variation can affect the ability to detect low dose effects in controlled studies."[4]

A review of the studies that were used to refute Hayes' research into the toxic effects of low doses of atrazine found many flaws in the design of the experiments. "Hayes' work also clearly addressed the so-called irreproducibility of these findings by analyzing the studies that were unable to find effects of the pesticide; he noted that the negative studies had multiple experimental flaws, including contamination of the controls with atrazine, overcrowding (and therefore underdosing) of experimental animals, and other problems with animal husbandry that led to mortality rates above 80%."[5]

> **THE PESTICIDE INDUSTRY** *has a long history of muddying the waters with false comparisons ... and has been very successful at convincing most people to believe the myth that their food is safe.*

These examples highlight the need to accurately replicate the material and methods used in the original studies when testing whether their results are credible rather than designing similar studies using variations of the materials and methods. In reality these "similar" studies are entirely new studies because they generally use a different set of criteria. Researchers are not replicating the original study, and therefore it should be expected that they will see different results than the original study.

Using studies that do not find adverse health effects to discredit and cast doubt on the credibility of a study that does, is a tactic used by some industries and regulators. Big Tobacco, the lead industry, and the asbestos industry did this for decades before public pressure working in partnership with concerned scientists finally forced the governments and regulatory authorities to implement some of the necessary changes. This inaction has resulted in and continues to cause millions of people to suffer from painful and needless illnesses and early deaths. Most recently this technique was used to sow the seeds of doubt about the science of human-created greenhouse gases as the major cause of climate change as well as junk food composed of empty calories as a cause of the global obesity epidemic.

The pesticide industry has a long history of muddying the waters with false comparisons like this and has been very successful at convincing most people to believe the myth that their food is safe.

ATTACKING THE MESSENGER

Another strategy used by the global Pesticide and GMOs corporations (they are mostly the same companies) is to attack the authors of the studies to discredit them as researchers and scientists. This is done by media campaigns that are designed to discredit the quality of the research and the people who did the research. Vandana Shiva, in the Foreword of this book, gives the example of these corporations going after independent scientists, such as Arpad Putzai, Tyron Hayes, Ignacio Chapela and Gilles-Éric Séralini to destroy their careers and credibility.

Vallianatos and Drucker give many examples in their books where industry pressure has destroyed the careers of researchers and suppressed good science that reveals the adverse health effects of GMOs and pesticides.

A very good example of how the chemical and GMO industries try to discredit scientists and corrupt the scientific processes is Professor Gilles-Éric Séralini's 2012 study, published in *Food and Chemical Toxicology*. This is the only peer-reviewed, lifetime (two years) comparison feeding study of a GMO and also for a formulated pesticide, in this case Roundup. The study found that rats fed a diet that contains a proportion of GM maize or minute residues of Roundup had significantly higher rates of kidney disease, liver damage, tumors and other negative health effects, including endocrine disruption.[6]

There are no regulatory requirements to test the safety of GMO foods as they are deemed to be "substantially equivalent" to their non-GMO counterparts based on a simple chemical analysis. No regulatory authority requires long-term chronic feeding studies for GMOs or for the formulated pesticides, such as Roundup, that are used in food production, although some companies voluntarily conduct ninety-day feeding trials of GMOs.

Previously, Dr. Séralini and colleagues reviewed nineteen of these ninety day GMO feeding studies that had concluded GMO foods were safe to eat. These studies cover more than 80 percent of the GMO varieties widely cultivated around the world. The review of these studies, published in *Environmental Sciences Europe*, found significant levels of negative effects to kidneys and livers in the animals that were fed GMOs. The scientists stated, "The kidneys were particularly affected, concentrating 43.5% of all disrupted parameters in males, whereas the liver was more specifically disrupted in females (30.8% of all disrupted parameters)."[7]

In order to have a better understanding of the long-term implications of eating GMOs and formulated pesticides, they decided to replicate a ninety-day feeding study conducted by Monsanto. Their review found disrupted health parameters, especially to liver and kidney function, in contrast to the conclusion by Monsanto that it was safe. The Monsanto researchers dismissed the findings as not biologically meaningful, and the European Food Safety Authority (EFSA) accepted Monsanto's interpretation on NK603 maize.

Séralini et al. decided to do a study over the lifetime of the animals (two years) to see if any problems occurred after ninety days. The Monsanto researchers adapted Guideline 408 of the Organisation for Economic Co-operation and Development (OECD) for their experimental design. This is regarded as excellent practice for toxicological studies, so consequently Séralini and his team used the same guideline.

They tested the same number and strain of rats per group as the Monsanto study to ensure an accurate comparison up to the ninety-day mark. They also wanted to see if it was the Roundup-tolerant GMO maize (NK603) or the Roundup pesticide that caused the health problems that they found in their review of original study. To determine this they added extra groups to the trials. The groups included rats being fed the NK603 with no Roundup and several groups of rats being fed NK603 maize with different levels of environmentally relevant residues of Roundup. The closest non-GMO strain of the maize was used for the control group, and the non-GMO maize with environmentally relevant levels of Roundup was used to test long-term effects of Roundup.

By comparing each group with the control group that only ate the non-GMO maize, they could see if there were any differences in health. If this was the case, they could determine if the health problems were caused by the GMO maize, the Roundup, or the combination of the GMO maize and Roundup.[8]

The results of the study found that the treated males displayed liver congestions and necrosis (dead tissue) at rates 2.5 to 5.5 times higher than the controls, as well as marked and severe kidney nephropathies (kidney damage) at rates generally 1.3 to 2.3 greater than the controls.

The study found that both GM maize and Roundup act as endocrine disrupters and their consumption resulted in female rats dying at a rate two to three times higher than the control animals. The pituitary gland was the second most disabled organ, and the sex hormonal balance was modified in females fed with the GMO and Roundup treatments. The pituitary gland is one of the master hormone glands, and its disruption can lead to a range of serious health problems.

THE STUDY FOUND *that both GM maize and Roundup act as endocrine disrupters and their consumption resulted in female rats dying at a rate two to three times higher than the control animals.*

Females that were fed either GM maize or non-GM maize with minute Roundup residues developed large mammary tumors almost always more often than and sooner than the controls. All the non-control females, except for one that had an ovarian tumor, had mammary hypertrophies (enlarged mammary glands) and in some cases hyperplasia with atypia (nodules in the mammary glands). These are generally considered precursors of cancer.

Treated males presented four times the number of tumors that were large enough to be felt by hand than the controls, and these occurred up to 600 days earlier.

Two of the important results were:

a. The non-monotonic endocrine-disrupting effects of Roundup in which the smallest levels were the most toxic;

b. the overexpression of the EPSPS transgene (a transgene is the gene that comes from another organism and is used to make the genetic modification) or other mutational effects in the GM maize, resulting in adverse metabolic consequences.

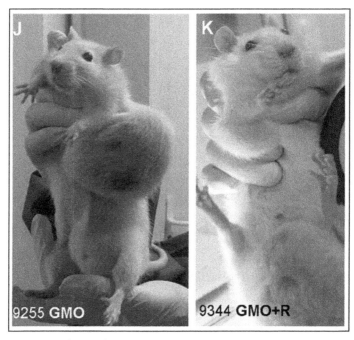

Source: Seralini et al.

These results have massive implications in that the non-monotonic effects of Roundup show that no dose is safe, especially the smallest residues. The implication that the overexpression of a transgene or other mutational effects caused by genetic modification are causing adverse metabolic changes such as liver and kidney damage and tumors reveals new mechanisms showing that all GMOs used for food could be causing widespread ill health.

Séralini and his colleagues concluded: "We propose that agricultural edible GMOs and formulated pesticides must be evaluated

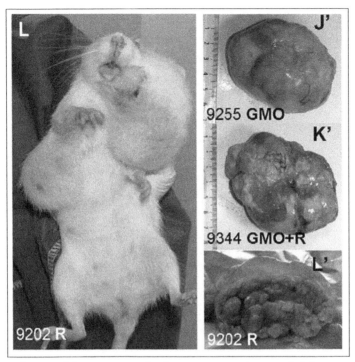

Images of the mammary gland tumors on rats that were fed the GMO maize, Roundup and GMO maize and Roundup.
Source Seralini et al.

very carefully by long term studies to measure their potential toxic effects."[9]

It is surprising that these products are used in food production with no long-term studies to measure their effects on health and no data to show that they are safe when consumed over a normal lifetime. This is a massive neglect of public safety by industry and regulators. Any reasonable person would agree that these studies must be done.

Seralinii's study is the only published lifetime study of a formulated pesticide. The fact that there have been no previous lifetime studies of the thousands of formulated pesticides used in the production of our food shows a serious neglect of science that is either incompetence or fraudulent collusion by the chemical industry and regulators. How can they say that any formulated pesticide used in our food is safe when they have not tested them over a lifetime of exposure? We are suppose to eat these toxic chemicals our whole lives with no evidence based science that they are safe. This is clearly a data free assumption that in the opinion of many can interpreted as incompetence, fraud or a combination of both by industry and regulators.

This study caused a huge controversy when it was first published in *Food and Chemical Toxicology* (FCT) in September 2012. Within the first week the pesticide and GMO industries started a huge campaign to discredit the study, including writing to the journal editor urging him to retract the article. The criticisms came mostly from plant biologists, without experience in toxicology, who were concerned that this study would affect their industry. Richard E. Goodman, a former employee of Monsanto, wrote the following in a letter to the editor-in-chief: "The implications and the impacts of this uncontrolled study is having HUGE impacts, in international trade, in consumer confidence in all aspects of food safety, and certainly in US state referendums on labeling."[10]

Despite Séralini and his coauthors answering all these criticisms in a paper published in FCT on November 9, 2012, an unrelenting campaign of potentially libelous comments appeared in different publications demanding the paper's retraction.[11]

Many people involved in this smear campaign have since been exposed as having undeclared links to GMO and pesticide industries and as having vested interests in GMO technology and patents. These links went largely undisclosed in media articles and in published letters to FCT; however, they were exposed by Séralini et al., investigative journalists, and organizations such as the Center for Public Integrity and U.S. Right to Know.[12]

Richard E. Goodman was appointed to the newly created post of associate editor for biotechnology for FCT. At the same time the former Editor for Europe for FCT, Dr. Jose L. Domingo, who had conducted the Seralini's study peer review was immediately forced out of the Journal. A. Wallace Hayes, the editor-in-chief of FCT, has admitted that Goodman was introduced into the editorial board after he sent a letter to FCT complaining about the Séralini study. Goodman asked for "an evaluation by an independent set of toxicologists" in his letter.[13] Consequently, Hayes had a second peer review done on the paper that did not find any major issues with it.

Hayes retracted the study on November 19, 2013. In his letter to Professor Séralini, Hayes stated that the data were not incorrect and that there was no misconduct, fraud or intentional misinterpretation of the data.

Hayes stated that no conclusions could be drawn because they tested ten rats per group, they used Sprague Dawley rats, and because the data were inconclusive on cancer.[14]

Séralini et al. never used the word "cancer" in the paper because the study was not proposed as a carcinogenicity study, which would require fifty rats per group under the OECD guidelines. It was a toxicological study and therefore used ten rats per group as required by the OECD guidelines for toxicological studies. Under the OECD guidelines for toxicological studies, the researchers must document and report all lesions. Tumors are lesions, so the reporting of tumors in this study met the OECD guidelines.

Sprague Dawley rats are industry standard for these types of studies because the way they develop tumors is similar to humans. Therefore they are regarded as a good model to test toxic substances for adverse health outcomes that may affect people.

The fact is that this study was done under the OECD guidelines for toxicological studies and the reviewers and the editor-in-chief acknowledged no evidence of fraud or intentional misrepresentation of the data. In reality, this study has been done to the highest standards, and its findings are conclusive for all of the negative effects, including tumors. Tumors are not the same as cancer; however, they can grow large enough where they disrupt the normal functioning of organs, causing ill health, internal hemorrhages, and most often death. Not all tumors are cancerous, as many can be benign and not lead to cancer. However, they are a hallmark of cancer and are rapidly more lethal in these cases.

Hayes' reasoning that the use of Sprague Dawley rats and only testing ten rats in each group meant that "the results presented (while not incorrect) are inconclusive, and therefore do not reach the threshold of publication for Food and Chemical Toxicology" would mean many published toxicological studies should be re-tracted.[15] In fact, many published studies do not use the OECD guidelines and are thus not as rigorous in methodology and results as the Séralini study.

Most significantly, the earlier ninety-day Monsanto study, which also used Sprague Dawley rats and tested ten rats in each group, was not retracted by the editor-in- chief of FCT. In fact, no other studies have been retracted on this basis.

Retracting a published study for inconclusive results would mean that thousands of scientific studies would have to be retracted, and it is very common for studies to have inconclusive results. Conse-quently, this fact alone is not a reason for retracting papers.

The grounds for retracting a paper have been outlined by the Committee on Publication Ethics (COPE). COPE states that the only grounds for retraction are (1) clear evidence that the findings are unreliable due to misconduct or honest error, (2) plagiarism or redundant publication, or (3) unethical research.

A 1990 PERFORMANCE RECORD *said one of Hayes' "objectives" was to "increase our knowledge base regarding the role of nicotine/cotinine in smoking enjoyment/ satisfaction."*

The Séralini paper meets none of these criteria and should not have been retracted. FCT as a member of COPE is supposed to abide by its rules. In this case, the rules have been ignored and the editor-in-chief has bowed to industry pressure and invented a new rule.

Not declaring a conflict of interest can be clear grounds for retraction due to misconduct. However, none of the letters the FCT published or the earlier Monsanto study where the authors did not declare a conflict of interest were retracted.

The fact is that the Séralini study met the OECD guidelines for good practice in toxicological studies, so the results are conclusive and significant.

Many people saw the retraction as a political decision and a cor-ruption of the objectivity of science that could not be scientifically or ethically justified. Numerous scientists were concerned that this decision was censorship of research into health risks and that it undermined the value, integrity, impartiality and the credibility of published science.

More than a hundred letters were written by scientists to the editor of Elsevier and the publisher of FCT in support of Séralini's study and the cause of independent science, asking for the retraction to be reversed. Two of the letters were open letters. One was signed by 1,402 scientists and 4,030 non-scientists from 100 different countries and the other by 182 scientists. Significantly more letters were written in support of the paper and the scientists than were written by the industry proponents to try and discredit the study.[17]

Various publications, especially on the internet, started to question the impartiality of the decision and featured articles showing the undeclared industry links to many of the people who wrote letters to the FCT to discredit the Séralini study and the scientists. They revealed that several members of the editorial board FCT have ties with the GMO and pesticide industry and/or to the International Life Sciences Institute (ILSI) that is funded by the GMO and Pesticide corporations.[18]

The appointment of ex-Monsanto employee Richard Goodman, an affiliate of ILSI, to the newly created post of associate editor for biotechnology at FCT, was seen as a conflict of interest and industry interference in the objectivity and impartiality of the journal.

The Center for Public Integrity revealed that A. Wallace Hayes, the editor-in-chief, served as an executive for RJR Nabisco, where he worked on both tobacco and food safety issues. A 1990 performance record said one of Hayes' "objectives" was to "increase our knowledge base regarding the role of nicotine/cotinine in smoking enjoyment/satisfaction."[19]

The retraction was seen as an example of an orchestrated campaign by industry proponents to discredit and suppress good science and credible scientists that they see as a threat to their business and profits. However, it did not work. The Séralini et al. study was republished in June 24, 2014 in *Environmental Sciences Europe* along with a second paper giving the details of the conflicts of interest of the various people who attacked the paper and also rebutting all of their allegations and misrepresentation.

As a result of all the negative comments and media, FCT and their editor-in-chief lost an enormous amount of credibility, especially when the study was republished. Hayes was quietly replaced as editor-in-chief by the previous editor of Seralini's paper, Dr Jose L. Domingo, and Goodman disappeared from the journal's editorial board. Under the new editor-in-chief, FCT has published papers showing that safety of GM crops is not an established fact.[20]

Séralini and his team successfully sued critics for defamation in two separate cases in the High Court of Paris. One of these critics was convicted by the High Court of France on the more serious charge of forging some of the "evidence" he was using to discredit Séralini et al.[21]

Professor Séralini was honored with the 2015 Whistleblower Award by the Federation of German Scientists and the German Section of the International Association of Lawyers Against Nuclear Arms for his unwavering refusal to abandon his professional ethics since the publication of his paper "gained him the worldwide support of many scientists who defended the methods he chose and deemed his research results to represent genuine scientific progress."[22]

Recording and reporting all the tumors in the rats, one of the reasons for the retraction, far from being inconclusive of cancer, has been validated with glyphosate being classified as a probable human carcinogen by the World Health Organization's IARC.

If the aim of the smear campaign, orchestrated by the GMO and pesticide industry, was to discredit this paper and make it disappear, then it is a spectacular case of a campaign backfiring. Instead of discrediting it and relegating it to the trash can of history, this paper has one of the highest profiles and has probably been read by more people than any other scientific paper in the last decade.

However, the industry dirty tricks campaign is still manipulating Wikipedia and internet blog sites against Séralini. They also went to see all the foundations and other financial institutions that support Séralini's research to discredit him and stop his funding. This has caused a range of financial and other difficulties for his university.

Despite this, Séralini still has his position as a highly respected professor and is publishing numerous scientific papers on this topic.

Over time, as more studies are published showing that GMOs and pesticide formulations cause numerous health problems, this study by Professor Séralini and his colleagues will be seen as a landmark study.

THE NEED FOR CHANGES IN THE METHODOLOGIES USED TO TEST CHEMICALS

One of the major issues repeated consistently in this book is the need for changes in the current approaches and methodologies used by regulatory authorities in assessing the safety of pesticides.

The huge body of missing information needs to be researched, and the outdated testing methods need to be augmented with the emerging body of scientific techniques so that they can provide the missing data.

Additional testing needs to be done for:

- Mixtures and cocktails of chemicals;
- The actual formulated products, not just the active ingredient;
- The toxicity of pesticide metabolites;
- The special requirements of fetuses, newborns, and growing children;
- Endocrine disruption;
- Metabolic disruption;
- Intergenerational effects on all organs and physiological systems;
- Developmental neurotoxicity; and
- Epigenetic damage.

Until this is done, regulatory bodies have no credible scientific evidence backing a statement that any level of pesticide residue is safe for humans or the environment.

DATA-FREE ASSUMPTIONS AS THE BASIS OF PESTICIDE REGULATION

The scientific credibility of pesticide regulatory authorities must be seriously questioned when they are approving the use of pesticides on the basis of data-free assumptions.

A good example of this is the approval of formulated pesticide products as safe on the basis of just testing one of the ingredients without testing the whole formulation. Given that the other chemical ingredients are chemically active as they are added to the formulations to make the active ingredient work more effectively, the assumption that they are inert and will not increase the toxicity of the whole formulation lacks scientific credibility. There are no requirements to test the toxicity of the whole formulation for adverse chronic health effects to generate credible evidence based scientific data. This means that the current approval process is based on the data-free assumption that the "inerts" do not alter the toxicity of the active ingredient.

Regulatory authorities approve several different pesticides for a crop—such as herbicides, fungicides, and insecticides—on the basis that all of them can be used in the normal production of the crop. Consequently, multiple residues will be found in the crop; residue testing found that 47.4 percent of food in the United States had two or more pesticide residues. The current approval process of testing each pesticide separately is based on the assumption that if each chemical is safe individually then the combinations of these chemicals are also safe. There are a number of published scientific studies showing that combinations of pesticide residues can cause serious adverse health outcomes due to additive or synergistic effects. The failure to test the combinations of approved pesticides for potential health risks means that regulatory authorities do not have any evidence-based data indicating that these residue combinations are safe. The current data-free assumption of safety used by regulatory authorities lacks scientific credibility.

The lack of testing for the metabolites of pesticides, given that limited testing shows that many of them are more toxic and residual than the pesticide itself, is another massive data gap. Once again, approval has been based on data-free assumptions of safety.

The setting of the ADI is another example. Given that there are hundreds of studies showing that many chemicals can be endocrine disruptors and therefore more toxic at lower doses, setting the ADI on the basis of extrapolating it from testing done at higher doses is another data-free assumption. The only way to ensure that the ADI is safe and does not act as an endocrine disruptor is to do the testing at the actual residue levels that are set for the ADI.

The special requirements of the fetus, the newborn, and the growing child in relation to developmental neurotoxicity are also subject to data-free assumptions. Currently the pesticide testing used in the regulatory approval processes does not specifically test for any of the risks particular to these age groups, and the ADIs are set based on the testing of adolescent animals. Until testing is specifically designed to assess the dangers to the developing fetus and the very young, there is no evidence-based data specific to this age group. Once again, pesticide ADIs are approved as safe for children without credible scientific evidence to prove their safety.

It is the same with intergenerational effects. Unless testing is done over several generations, especially on organs and physiological processes, these is no data to show that the current ADIs will not cause health problems for the future generations. There are many scientific studies showing that exposure to pesticide residues cause adverse health problems in future generations, so ignoring this issue could prove dangerous. It is a data-free assumption to approve pesticides on the basis that these intergenerational effects are not a significant issue.

Similarly, there has been no testing for damage to the epigenome despite the numerous scientific papers showing how pesticides cause epimutations and that many of these can be inherited for several generations.

Without doing the scientific research to generate the evidence-based data, regulatory authorities are making safety decisions in a vacuum of evidence.

One of the greatest concerns is the lack of action by regulators when published research shows the harm that pesticides are doing.

The lack of action on glyphosate by major regulators such as the US EPA and EFSA is an example.

The regulation of pesticides should be based on data generated through credible scientific studies and testing, not on data-free assumptions as it is currently.

THE POSITIVE ALTERNATIVE AND FUTURE

Even if regulatory authorities started tomorrow, it would take decades and billions of dollars in funds to test all the registered pesticide products and the thousands of common combinations to acquire the relevant missing data needed to establish the safe use of these poisons.

In the meantime a precautionary approach to avoid pesticides is the best strategy because reducing pesticide exposure to lower levels gives no guarantee of safety. Currently, due to the numerous significant data gaps, there is no credible science to show that any level of residue is safe. Adopting farming systems that replace pesticides with nontoxic, natural methods of pest control is the most effective and logical way to avoid the current uncertainties surrounding pesticide use.

Research has clearly shown that regenerative organic agriculture can get the yields needed to feed the poor and the hungry, especially in the case of smallholder agriculture—the majority of the world's farmers.

It is critically important that a substantial proportion of the billions of dollars spent on research and development of chemically intensive agriculture are invested on researching the possibilities of the emerging high-yielding organic systems. Using research and development to replicate, improve, and scale these systems up globally will enable agriculture to achieve high yields without the use of toxic chemicals.

REDUCED PESTICIDE USE MAKES NO DIFFERENCE IN SAFETY

There are many certified food-labeling systems that portray themselves as ecological or sustainable because of reduced pesticide use and perpetuate the myth of "safe food." In the case of "good agricultural practices," all pesticides permitted by regulators can be used as long as they are used according to the label on the container. The assumption is that as long as the pesticides are used per the label's instructions, they are safe.

Some of these "sustainability label" systems use the WHO's toxicity classification as the basis of safe use. They prohibit the use of the most acutely toxic chemicals based on the LD_{50}s, but they allow the use of thousands of other toxic pesticide formulations. As stated in chapter 1, LD_{50}s are used to determine the acute toxicity of a chemical (the toxicity that will quickly cause death) but are irrelevant in showing the longer-term toxic effects (slow poison) of a chemical or formulated mixtures, such as cancers, cell mutations, endocrine disruption, birth defects, organ and tissue damage, nervous system damage, behavior changes, epigenetic damage, and immune system damage.

Other "safe-food," "sustainable," and "eco-label" systems just prohibit pesticides banned by the European Union (EU) and/or the United States; however, as has been shown repeatedly throughout this book, the vast majority of the thousands of chemicals used in the EU and the United States have not been tested for safety. This is especially the case with the thousands of commercial pesticide formulations composed of the active ingredient and the "inerts" that have no testing for the numerous adverse health effects that peer-reviewed scientific papers have linked to pesticides. Consumers should therefore be greatly concerned that thousands of these formulations are permitted in "safe-food," "good-agricultural-practice," "sustainable," and "eco-label" certification systems.

These systems cannot give any guarantee that their pesticide use is any safer than conventional systems while they permit the use of any level of synthetic chemical pesticides. Given that the science shows that for many chemicals even the smallest amounts can have serious adverse health effects, especially on the developing fetus and growing children, any residues are potentially unsafe, no matter how small. In these situations, reduced amounts make no difference. In many ways, these eco/sustainable label claims are confusing consumers who assume that they are virtually organic in that they use few or no pesticides, when in reality the opposite is true. These non-organic label schemes permit thousands of toxic pesticide formulations.

GENUINE ORGANIC LABELING SYSTEMS

The fact is that only genuine organic labeling systems can guarantee that food is produced without pesticides. There are a variety of credible ways to guarantee the integrity of the organic produce. Many countries utilize government-regulated schemes such as those run by the USDA or EU where a third-party inspector certifies the product. Some countries offer a range of participatory guarantee systems (PGS) that involve groups of farmers, and often they include groups of consumers. PGSs are based on standards and a peer-review system that ensures that all the members of the group comply with the standard. Some countries, such as South Korea or Japan, have large co-ops of farmers and consumers. These co-ops have their own standards and systems for checking the integrity of all the organic products that they produce and sell. Some of the fastest growing credible systems are organic consumer supported agriculture (CSA) programs. As a member of a CSA, consumers pay the farmer an advance fee for produce. CSAs are one of the best ways for consumers and farmers to connect to buy and sell fresh, local, high-quality, seasonal produce. Because the consumers can have regular access to the farm, they can see with their own eyes if toxic chemicals are being used. Another option is to purchase produce from farmers markets that check their farmers' production claims.

The critical issue is to look at how the claims about any food can be verified. It is worthwhile to do a little bit of homework to check the accuracy of the label claims before spending money.

HEALTH MUST COME FIRST

Out of all the criteria being used to assess the environmental sustainability of agricultural systems, the health of people and all the biodiverse forms of life in our planet's ecosystems must be our number one priority.

What are the major benefits of having good recycling outcomes, low-carbon footprints, low energy use, better water-use efficiency, locally grown produce, natural, etc., if the production system is severely harming the health of the surrounding environment and the people who consume the products from it? It is an even greater concern when the genetic damage caused by pesticides propagates a harmful legacy that will be passed onto future generations.

Is it better to have the freshness of locally grown produce that is toxic or a nontoxic product that may not be as fresh? Ideally it is best to have fresh, locally grown, and nontoxic, but when the ideal isn't available it is always better to have nontoxic as the first choice. People do not get serious illnesses because of the difference in the distance a product has traveled to get to market. On the other hand there can be serious consequences from even minute chemical residues in the food consumed by mothers being passed through the placenta to the fetus or through breast milk to the newborn, even if it is locally produced.

It is the same with all the other ecological options. Ideally we want good environmental outcomes across all criteria; however when the ideal isn't possible, the health of our future generations must come first. How can we pass on a better world to them when we are passing on generations of adverse health outcomes?

ORGANIC FOOD IS HEALTHIER

The largest and most comprehensive peer-reviewed scientific study comparing organic food and conventional food was published in *British Journal of Nutrition* by a team of international experts under the auspices of Newcastle University, UK. It clearly established that organic foods are more nutritious. This meta-study analyzed 343 published peer-reviewed studies and found that levels of antioxidants were between 18 and 69 percent higher in organic food compared to conventional food. The study showed that the levels

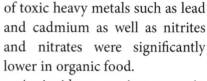

THE STUDY ANALYZED OVER 37,000 WOMEN *and their children and found that women who said they had consumed some organic food during pregnancy were less likely to give birth to a boy with hypospadias compared to those who said that they seldom or never ate organic food.*

of toxic heavy metals such as lead and cadmium as well as nitrites and nitrates were significantly lower in organic food.

Antioxidants are important in preventing oxidative stress. Oxidative stress is one of the hallmarks of cancer and a contributing factor to many chronic diseases. It's caused by an imbalance between free radicals and the body's ability to repair the damage caused by free radicals. Free radicals damage many types of body cells and tissues by oxidizing them. Antioxidants "mop up" the damaging free radical compounds, preventing them from doing damage. Numerous scientific studies show multiple benefits of diets rich in antioxidants because of their protective benefits in preventing and reducing cardiovascular disorders, neurodegenerative disorders, autoimmune disorders, premature aging, cancers, and numerous other diseases.

The meta-study by the Newcastle University team analyzed significantly more studies than previous ones, such as those done by Stanford University and the 2009 UK Food Standards Agency that only looked at forty-six studies. Both of these previous studies concluded there were no significant nutritional differences between organic and conventional food despite finding, like the Newcastle University study, that organic food had higher levels of antioxidants.

The extensive analysis of 343 studies done for the Newcastle University study shows that there is no doubt that organic food is healthier and more nutritious.[23]

PROTECTING OUR CHILDREN AND FUTURE

The most logical strategy to reduce our children's' exposure to pesticides is to avoid them as much as possible. This isn't rocket science, and it's very easy to do. For the majority of people, most of our exposure to pesticides comes from food, followed by pesticides used in the house as insect sprays and in the garden. There are many simple, effective, nontoxic, natural ways to control bugs in the house, and numerous good books are available on this subject. Similarly, pesticides aren't needed to control bugs and weeds in the garden, and once again, many useful books on this subject are available.

Currently for consumers, the best way to avoid the bulk of these poisons is to eat organically grown food that has been produced with organic guarantee systems such as third-party certification, participatory guarantee systems (PGS), as a member of an organic CSA scheme, or farmers markets that check their farmers' production claims. These guarantee systems will ensure that the food is produced without toxic compounds. Most importantly, many scientific studies show that eating organic food results in significantly lower levels of these pervasive chemicals in humans, particularly children.

New research is showing that by eating organic food, women can protect the health of their children before they are born. A large epidemiological study, published in *Environmental Health Perspectives*, found that the consumption of organic food resulted in baby boys with decreased rates of hypospadias (penile malformations) and cryptorchidism (undescended testes), both common types of male urogenital birth defects. The study analyzed over 37,000 women and their children and found that women who said they had consumed some organic food during pregnancy were less likely to give birth to a boy with hypospadias compared to those who said that they seldom or never ate organic food.

This finding is significant as the WHO-UNEP meta-study on endocrine disruptors found an increase in urogenital malformations in baby boys, such as undescended testes and penile malformations. The study in *Environmental Health Perspectives* shows that eating organic food can protect against the negative effects of endocrine disruptors.[24]

Another study published in *Environmental Health Perspectives* found that children who eat organic fruits, vegetables, and juices can significantly lower the levels of organophosphate pesticides in their bodies. The University of Washington researchers who conducted the study concluded, "The dose estimates suggest that consumption of organic fruits, vegetables, and juice can reduce children's exposure levels from above to below the U.S. Environmental Protection Agency's current guidelines, thereby shifting exposures from a range of uncertain risk to a range of negligible risk. Consumption of organic produce appears to provide a relatively simple way for parents to reduce their children's exposure to OP [organophosphate] pesticides."[25]

Researchers in a 2006 study found that the urinary concentrations of the specific metabolites for malathion and chlorpyrifos decreased to undetectable levels immediately after the introduction of organic diets and remained undetectable until the conventional diets were reintroduced. The researchers from Emory University, Atlanta, Georgia; the University of Washington, Seattle, Washington; and the Centers for Disease Control and Prevention, Atlanta, Georgia, stated, "In conclusion, we were able to demonstrate that an organic diet provides a dramatic and immediate protective effect against exposures to organophosphorus pesticides that are commonly used in agricultural production. We also concluded that these children were most likely exposed to these organophosphorus pesticides exclusively through their diet."[26]

WHAT IS THE TRUE COST OF FOODS THAT CONTAIN POISON RESIDUES?

It is time to dispense with the myth that foods from farming systems that use synthetic pesticides are safe to eat. This includes low- or reduced-pesticide farming systems, as there is no credible science to guarantee that any level of exposure is safe. The lack of rigorous testing and the blatant disregard of the current science by regulators means that, until these data gaps are filled, the most logical option is to avoid food from farming systems that use these toxic compounds.

Some people complain about the cost of organic food. However, what is the true cost of foods that contain poison residues? No amount of money can undo the damage that small amounts of pesticides are doing to our children.

The most important question is, "How much is the health of our children worth?" As parents, we have a duty of care to give our children the best start in life, and good health is one of the most important factors. Purchasing and eating organic food is one of the cheapest and most effective ways to ensure the best start in life for our children.

NOTES

[1] Dan Fagin, "Toxicology: The Learning Curve," *Nature* 490, no. 7421 (October 2012): 462–65.

[2] Vandenberg et al., "Hormones and Endocrine-Disrupting Chemicals."

[3] Fagin, "Toxicology."

[4] Vandenberg et al., "Hormones and Endocrine-Disrupting Chemicals."

[5] Ibid.

[6] Séralini et al., "Long-Term Toxicity of a Roundup Herbicide."

[7] Gilles-Éric Séralini, Robin Mesnage, E. Clair, S. Gress, Joël Spiroux de Vendomois, and D. Cellier, "Genetically Modified Crops Safety Assessments: Present Limits and Possible Improvements," *Environmental Sciences Europe* 23 (2011): 10.

[8] Gilles-Éric Séralini, Robin Mesnage, Nicolas Defarge, and Joël Spiroux de Vendômois, "Conflicts of Interests, Confidentiality and Censorship in Health Risk Assessment: The Example of an Herbicide and a GMO," *Environmental Sciences Europe* 26 (2014): 13, http://www.enveurope.com/content/26/1/13.

[9] Gilles-Éric Séralini, Emilie Clair, Robin Mesnage, Steeve Gress, Nicolas Defarge, Manuela Malatesta, Didier Hennequin, Joël Spiroux de Vendômois, "Long Term Toxicity of a Roundup Herbicide."

[10] Séralini et al., "Conflicts of Interests, Confidentiality and Censorship."

[11] Gilles-Éric Séralini, Robin Mesnage, Nicolas Defarge, S. Gress, D. Hennequin, E. Clair, M. Malatesta, Joël Spiroux de Vendomois, "Answers to Critics: Why There Is a Long Term Toxicity Due to NK603 Roundup-Tolerant Genetically Modified Maize and to a Roundup Herbicide," *Food and Chemical Toxicology* 53 (2013): 461–68.

[12] Séralini et al., "Conflicts of Interests, Confidentiality and Censorship."

[13] Ibid.

[14] A. Wallace Hayes, Retraction Letter to Professor Séralini, November 19, 2013, http://www.gmwatch.org/files/Letter_AWHayes_GES.pdf.

[15] Hayes, Retraction Letter to Professor Séralini.

[16] Séralini et al., "Conflicts of Interests, Confidentiality and Censorship."

[17] "Scientists Support Séralini: Introduction," GMOSeralini.org, http://www.gmoseralini.org/introduction-to-scientists-support-seralini/; "Open Letter on Retraction and Pledge to Boycott Elsevier," Institute of Science in Society, April 12, 2013, http://www.i-sis.org.uk/Open_letter_to_FCT_and_Elsevier.php; "Journal Retraction of Séralini GMO Study Is Invalid and an Attack on Scientific Integrity," End Science Censorship, http://www.endsciencecensorship.org/en/page/Statement#signed-by.

[18] Christoph Then, "Economic Interests Quashing Scientific Controversy?," TestBiotech, November 29, 2013, http://www.testbiotech.org/node/972.

[19] Chris Young and Erin Quinn, "Food Safety Scientists Have Ties to Big Tobacco," Center for Public Integrity, April 15, 2015, http://www.publicintegrity.org/2015/04/15/17144/food-safety-scientists-have-ties-big-tobacco.

[20] Ibid.

[21] "Séralini's Team Wins Defamation and Forgery Court Cases on GMO and Pesticide Research," GMOSeralini.org, November 27, 2015, http://www.gmoseralini.org/seralinis-team-wins-defamation-and-forgery-court-cases-on-gmo-and-pesticide-research/.

[22] "Federation of German Scientists Whistleblower Award Goes to Prof Gilles-Eric Séralini," GMOSeralini.org, October 23, 2015, http://www.gmoseralini.org/federation-of-german-scientists-whistleblower-award-goes-to-prof-gilles-eric-seralini/.

[23] M. Baranski et al., "Higher Antioxidant Concentrations and Less Cadmium and Pesticide Residues in Organically-Grown Crops: A Systematic Literature Review and Meta-Analyses," *British Journal of Nutrition*, July 15, 2014.

[24] Anne Lise Brantsæter, Hanne Torjusen, Helle Margrete Meltzer, Eleni Papadopoulou, Jane A. Hoppin, Jan Alexander, Geir Lieblein, Gun Roos, Jon Magne Holten, Jackie Swartz and Margaretha Haugen, "Organic Food Consumption during Pregnancy and Hypospadias and Cryptorchidism at Birth: The Norwegian Mother and Child Cohort Study (MoBa)," *Environmental Health Perspectives*, July 9, 2015, http://dx.doi.org/10.1289/ehp.1409518.

[25] Cynthia Curl, Richard A. Fenske, and Kai Elgethun, "Organophosphorus Pesticide Exposure of Urban and Suburban Preschool Children with Organic and Conventional Diets," *Environmental Health Perspectives* 111, no. 3 (March 2003): 377–82.

[26] Chensheng Lu et al., "Organic Diets Significantly Lower Children's Dietary Exposure to Organophosphorus Pesticides," *Environmental Health Perspectives* 114, no. 2 (February 2006): 260–63.

Index

chemical cocktails, 3–9. *See also* additive effects;
      synergistic interactions
Chemical-Management Policy: Prioritizing Children's Health, 23,
      86–87
chemical weapons, 27
childhood cancers, 97
   rates, 25–26
   children
   pesticide exposure in, 24–25, 182–184
   vulnerability to pesticide toxicity, 23, 159–160
Chile, 116
China, 117
chlordane, 74
chlorinated pesticides, 19, 77–80
chlorpyrifos, 22, 27, 29, 76, 117
   ban on, 34, 117, 118
   metabolites of, 74, 75
   prenatal exposure to, 31, 33
   climate change, xxxi, 126, 127, 128–131, 137–138, 144
   organic agriculture's resilience in, 136–142
Colborn, Theo, xxx, 24–25, 28, 76, 88, 119
colorectal cancer, 61
Columbia University Center for Children's Environmental
      Health, 31
Committee on Publication Ethics (COPE), 172
compost, 143, 144
Compost Utilization Trial, 131
conflicts   of   interest,   of   regulatory   authorities,   89–90,   92–93,
      114–115, 172
consumer-supported agriculture (CSA), 180, 183
Cornell University, 134
corticosterone, 100
cortisol, 100
Critical Reviews in Toxicology, 114
cytochrome P450 (CYP), 15, 99–101

D

2,4-D, 18–19, 67, 76, 77, 78, 79, 80
DDT, 36, 73, 86, 117
DEET, 41–42
dehydroepiandrosterone, 103
Delate, Kathleen, 134–135
depression, 35, 68–69
desmodium, 150–151, 152–153
developing world
   regulatory authorities in, 84–85
   smallholder farms in, 140–144, 178
developmental neurotoxicity, 28–40, 103
diabetes, 58, 59–60, 68–69, 106, 109, 110
diazinon, 29, 74, 75
dicamba, 8, 67
dichlorophenols, 76–77
dichlorvos, 76

environmental effects, of pesticides, xxix–xxx

Environmental Health Perspectives, 8, 24–25, 29, 34, 67, 68, 95, 183

environmentally relevant, definition of, 5

Environmental Protection Agency (EPA), 1, 67, 160
  bisphenol A study, 162–163
  glyphosate regulations, 92, 109–110
  influence of pesticide industry on, 87–88, 109–110
  National Pesticide Information Center, 92–95
  organophosphate exposure guidelines, 183–184
  Pesticide Data Program, 39, 83
  Pesticide Disrupter Screening Program, 83–87
  pesticides registered by, 2
  pesticide use monitoring role, 85
  Toxic Substance Control Act administration by, 86–87
  Voluntary Children's Chemical Evaluation Program, 87

Environmental Sciences Europe, 99, 166, 173

Environmental Working Group, 3, xxvi

EPA. *See* Environmental Protection Agency

epigenetics, 9–10, 11, 41–42, 177

Eriksson, Mikael, 97

estradiol, 4–5

estrogen-mimicking effects, of pesticides, 55

estrogens, 57, 100
  artificial, 4–5
  as breast cancer risk factor, 5, 65–66
  fetal developmental effects, 64–66

ETC Group, 141

Ethiopia, Tigray Project, 143–144

Europe, 7–8

European Commission, 70, 93

European Food Safety Authority (EFSA), 37–38, 90, 93, 109–110, 116, 166

European Union, 8, 85, 89–100, 110, 118, 179, 180
  Registration, Evaluation, and Authorization of Chemicals (REACH), 115–116

EXTOXNET (Extension Toxicology Network), 94–95

F

Fagin, Dan, 162–163

FAO (Food and Agriculture Organization), 141, 142

farmers' markets, 180, 183

FASEB Journal, 36–37

Federation of German Scientists, 174

Feminization of Nature, The (Cadbury), xxx

fertilizers, 6–7, 77, 130

fetus
  chlorpyrifos exposure in, 31
  effect of chemical metabolites on, 81
  epigenetic effects on, 41–42
  GMO-produced toxins in, 12
  pesticide exposure in, 24–25
  vulnerability to endocrine disrupters, 52–53, 64–65
  vulnerability to pesticides, 28–29, 159–160

N

NASA, 136
National Cancer Institute, 2
National Institute of Environmental Health Sciences (NIEHS), 79
National Institutes of Health, 2
National Pesticide Information Center, 94–95
National Toxicology Program, 163–164
National Toxics Network, 118
Natural minerals, 147
Nature, 67, 132–133, 135, 162
neonicotinoids, 26, 37–40, 81
 degradation of, 38–39
 effect on children, 39–40
 metabolites of, 77
 toxicity to birds and wildlife, 37–38
nerve gases/poisons, 26–27, 36, 39
nervous system
 damage to, 6–7, 28–40
 development, 11
neurobehavioral disorders, 59
neurotoxicity, developmental, 28–40, 103
NeuroToxicology, 103
newborn infants
 toxic chemical levels in, 3–4
 vulnerability to endocrine disrupters, 64
 vulnerability to pesticides, 28–29
Newcastle University, 181, 182
New Zealand, 73
nicotine, 40, 173
nitrate fertilizers, 6–7
nitrogen fertilizers, 130
nitrous oxide, 130
non-Hodgkin's lymphoma, 91, 97, 109
no observed effect (NOAEL), 53, 56
nutrient deficiencies, 145–146, 147

O

obesity, 58, 59, 67, 68–69, 105, 109, 142
OECD (Organisation for Economic Co-operation and
  Development), 166, 171–172
omethoate, 27, 75–76
Oregon State University, 94–95
organ development, 96–97
organic agriculture, xxx–xxxi, 178
 carbon sequestration in, 129, 130–131
 climate change and, 128–131
 comparison with conventional agriculture, 129, 130–131,
  132–144
 effect on biodiversity, 128
 nutrients supplied by, 145–146
 organic pesticides in, 146–153
 research funding for, 132, 133, 152, 153–154, 178
 resilience in adverse conditions, 136–142

somatrophin, 57
South Africa, 116
Southern Illinois University, 74
South Korea, 116, 180
soybeans, 5–6, 66
sprays
    botanical, 148
    nontoxic, 147
Sri Lanka, 102
Stanford University, 182
State of the Science of Endocrine Disrupting Chemicals 2012, 4–5
Steiner, Achim, 141
Storrs, Sarah, 67
sustainability, 125–128, 180–181
Swanson, Nancy, 89–90, 103–107, 110–111
Sweden, 97
Switzerland, 7, 117
    Research Institute of Organic Agriculture (FiBL), 139, 140
synergistic interactions, 4–9, 10–11, 13
    implication for toxicity testing, 18–21
synergists, 15–16
Syngenta, 110–111
systemic pesticides, 39, 75

T

2,4,5-T, 78
teratogenicity. *See* birth defects
testicular cancer, 59
testicular disorders, 42, 67–68
testosterone, 57, 100
2,3,7,8-tetrachlorobidenzo-p-dioxin (TCDD), 19, 78, 79
Thailand, 116
Third World Network (TWN), 144
thyroid cancer, 59, 104, 108
thyroid disorders, 8, 88
thyroid-stimulating hormones, 57
Tigray Project, 143–144
Tilman, David, 126
Times Beach, Missouri, 79
tobacco industry, 162, 164, 173
toxicity testing
    adverse outcomes in, 161–162, 164–165
    based on data-free assumptions, 175–177
    dose-response model, 59
    of GMO foods, 165–173
    inadequacies and limitations of, 2–3, 4, 14–21, 52, 80–81, 163–164
    lack of applicability to children, xxviii, 23–40, 31, 33–34, 43, 160
    lifetime exposure studies, 165–175
    limitations of, 85–86
    low-dose hypothesis of, 53, 55–56, 68, 69
    need for changes in, 175
    non-governmental, 26
    no observed effect (NOAEL) in, 56, 5253

OECD guidelines for, 171–172
"representative samples," 80
scientifically unsound methodology in, 18–21
single-agent, 13
toxicology
definition of, 55
father of, 55
Toxicology, 95
Toxicology and Industrial Health, 6–7
Toxic Substance Control Act (TSCA), 23, 86–87
transgenes, 168

U
Uganda, 117
UNEP. *See* United Nations Environmental Programme (UNEP)
United Kingdom, 25
Food Standards Agency, 182
Health and Safety Executive, 17
United Nations (UN)
Chemical Weapons Convention, 27
Conference on Trade and Development (UNCTAD), 140–141
Development Programme (UNDP), 126
Educational, Scientific and Cultural Organization (UNESCO), 126
Environment Programme (UNEP), 4–5, 43, 52, 56, 126, 140–141
Food and Agriculture Organization (FAO), 126, 141, 142
Framework Convention on Climate Change, 136
Millennium Ecosystem Assessment Synthesis Report, 125–126
United States, 116
U.S. Agricultural Research Service (ARS) Pecan Trial, 133
U.S. Department of Agriculture, 80, 108
Pesticide Data Program, 1, 39, 83, 108
U.S. Department of Health and Human Services, 2
U.S. Food and Drugs Administration, 163
U.S. Geological Survey, 7, 74
U.S. President's Cancer Panel (USPCP), 2–3, 13, 14, 23–24, 25, 43, 61, 69, 74, 77, 89, 119, xxvii
University of California, 31, 126
University of Illinois, 130
University of Michigan, 141
University of Southern Denmark, 34
University of Victoria, 96
University of Washington, 183–184
University of Wisconsin-Madison, 6–7
urinary/bladder cancer, 106, 108
USPCP. *See* United States President's Cancer Panel (USPCP)
U.S. Right to Know, 170

V
Vallianatos, Evaggelos, 14, 15, 19, 78, 87–88, 90, 91, 165
Vandenberg, Laura N., 162–164
veterinary medicines, 132
Vietnam, 78–80
vinclozolin, 41
vom Saal, Frederick, 163